MACGREGOR'S FINAL BATTLE

JOE CLARK

"The spirit of a warrior is not geared to indulging and complaining, nor is it geared to winning or losing. The spirit of a warrior is geared only to struggle, and every struggle is a warrior's last battle on earth. Thus the outcome matters very little to him. In his last battle on earth a warrior lets his spirit flow free and clear."

A Separate Reality **by Carlos Castaneda**

1

He turned onto the ramp and followed signs to the restaurants. He needed a break. He had needed a break for the last few hours. A small place with a weathered look caught his attention. Its clapboard facade gave the impression the establishment had been there since the Civil War and Parkersburg had grown up around it. My Country Kitchen, the name on the sign above the entrance, was enough to get him to give it a try.

He struggled to his feet, his thigh muscles balking at the sudden call to action. He had to warm them up before he could make his way to the camper's door and climb down to the parking lot. Once on the asphalt, he stood, hands on the small of his back, and stretched. Food services and gas stations lined both sides of the road. He lumbered to the entrance of the little joint, hips and knees complaining with every step.

He paused inside the door. The place had a relaxed, homey feel. There was no hostess. He half expected someone to call out, "C'mon in and make yerself t' home."

A dozen or more oaken tables were available in the sparsely populated dining area. Four placemats with silverware wrapped in a napkin and an upside-down coffee cup on a saucer had been set out on each table.

The man made his way to a table in the back next to the wall on the left side of the room and took a seat facing the entrance. He thought of himself as a pariah – tossed aside by the world. He was in no mood for company.

A bubbly young woman with a pot of coffee came over and filled his cup. "Welcome to Mah Country Kitchen. Would y'all lak a menu, or do y'all know what y'all want?"

That was enough to shock him back to reality. The dark layer he had constructed as a shield blew apart. A dazzling goddess stood before him, demanding attention in a flat, nasal twang.

How am I supposed to know? rattled through his brain but no words came out. The waitress tilted her head and raised her eyebrows. He cleared his throat. A bit of phlegm pushed into his mouth. He swallowed it. Finally, he growled, "I want breakfast."

"Yeah, suh," she drawled sounding like she had grown up in West Virginia. "Eggs, pancakes, waffles, creamed beef, chitlins, grits. Y'all name it. We got it."

He toyed with some ideas that might challenge her but ended up asking for something safe. "Eggs. Sunny-side-up. Sausage. Toast. Whole Wheat."

"Two eggs or three?"

"Three."

The waitress nodded. She tipped her head toward a door across the room. "Would y'all lak a paper?"

Newspapers and magazines lay in a haphazard pile on a table near the door to the kitchen. "You got the New York Times?" he croaked. His vocal cords hadn't fully warmed up.

"Ah'm sure we do."

She set her coffee pot down on the table and sashayed over to fetch a paper. The man studied her approvingly. A pink dress came halfway down her tan, well-toned thighs. Her prominent breasts looked firm but not overly large. Her shapely butt begged to be handled.

She returned with a copy of the Times. It had been taken apart, read, and reassembled. The waitress smiled brightly as she held it out to him. "Fresh off the press."

That had to be a joke. He grinned. "Thanks."

"No problem. Ah'll be raht back with yer eggs."

Newspapers are better than TV news programs. They give more information. Magazines top newspapers. They provide lengthy, well-written pieces on important issues. All of them – magazines, newspapers, and TV – talk about the same stuff. And they all emphasize the titillating, lurid, gory details.

The front page of his paper featured stories about strikes by public transportation employees and teachers in New York City. A story about a top administration official misusing public funds got a headline. Toward the back of the front section, an op-ed piece raged about the latest international crisis created by the president.

He scanned the room playing spy while pretending to read his newspaper. There were three couples eating meals. Two appeared to be locals who had come from the office for lunch. The third was a man and a woman dressed for vacation. She wore a broad-brimmed, protective straw hat. Her sleeveless dress was canary yellow. His shirt was covered with beach scenes on a red background. Both of them sported sunglasses. The man's Aviators sat on a bald spot just above his round forehead.

No sign of the good-looking brunette with his breakfast. A woman in a black sweater seated across the aisle from him looked interesting. She was busy with something on her laptop. The dishes had been removed from her table. Reference materials were spread around her computer, but she never used them.

He skipped to the Sports section. More disappointment. Pedestrian thoughts couched in overly formal language appropriate to a bygone era. The stories read like PhD dissertations on trivial events.

His attention returned to the woman across the aisle. She looked to be about fifty. Her dark skin could be the kind that never aged. A white streak ran down the middle of her coal-black hair. She leaned back to take a break from her typing and caught him staring.

Some women complain that men undress them. Women strip men bare to their souls. She held his gaze for a long time before breaking the silence with her throaty contralto. "Don't be a stranger. Come on over and introduce yourself."

The man's cheeks reddened. He put his paper down and picked up his coffee to join her. She closed her laptop and extended a hand. "Tereza."

"Donald." He took her hand. "Donald MacGregor."

"Ah. A Scot and a member of *that* clan."

He had been told his ancestry traced back to the Scottish outlaw Rob Roy, but he'd never given it much thought. "That was a long time ago. Things are different now. We don't engage in cattle raids these days."

"For gypsies as well. But I have inherited powers from my ancestors."

"*Powers*? Something in your DNA gives you *powers*?"

"I doubt you'll find anything in my DNA, but the fact is I have rare abilities."

"For example?"

"Said like a true Scot. You are descended from hard-headed realists. That makes you a good engineer but leaves you spiritually impoverished."

"Spirituality is for fools who can't deal with reality."

"Spirituality is what enables us to live with what you think of as reality."

"In the end, it's an empty promise," he fumed.

"And yet you are on a spiritual journey."

"I'm going to visit a cousin."

"Because you are lost and alone?"

"Because I've got nothing better to do."

"Or because your wife left you?" Tereza suggested.

"She died!" MacGregor snapped.

"She's right here with us," the gypsy countered. She nodded toward the chair to his left. "A beautiful woman with a warm smile. She knows you are a fool, but she loves you for your strength and courage."

"You're guessing," he bristled. "You don't know anything about my wife."

"Most people call you 'Don'. She called you 'Mac' because, to her, you were a MacGregor."

Abandoned memories surfaced. His head bowed. His eyes closed. Anne had called him 'Donald', when they were first going together. Sometimes she called him "Laird," usually in a tone dripping with sarcasm. For the most part, he was "Mac."

Tereza took his hands. "She didn't die. She passed on. And your time is at hand. It's okay. We are not meant to be here forever."

That hit him like an electric shock. Tereza watched with a quiet, reassuring smile. "Do you want to tell me about it?"

A vision of Anne popped into his head. She had just stumbled as she crossed the kitchen. She blushed and giggled. "I must be entering my second childhood," she had joked, "I haven't done that for years."

That brought a smile to his face. "It was sudden," he began. "One day she was full of life. The next, she was lying unconscious in a hospital bed. She didn't speak or move. Nothing happened when I took her hand. The next day I was making funeral arrangements."

Tereza nodded.

"We buried her. Friends stopped by or called to see if I was okay. I told them I was adjusting."

His breakfast finally arrived. The pretty young waitress set it in front of him and asked if he wanted more coffee. MacGregor smiled up at her and shook his head. "Nah. I'm fine. But thank you for asking."

Her face brightened. "Yeah, suh." She handed him a bill. "Y'all can pay on yer way out."

He sipped his coffee while he gathered his thoughts. "My doctor had asked me to come in to talk about my last physical. Anne got sick before I got around to it. I wanted to put it off for a couple of weeks after the funeral. He insisted I had to come in as soon as possible."

Mac took another sip of coffee. It was getting cold. He regretted not taking the refresh. He grimaced. "It was a long day. Blood tests, urine sample, and a CAT scan. Then I sat down with the doctor. He told me I had a brain tumor and it might not be operable. He was going to have an expert evaluate the data. That would take a few days." Mac closed his eyes and shook his head. "I was pretty sure what the expert was going to say."

He looked up at the ceiling and took a deep breath before pushing on. "When I got home, I could tell something was wrong. Rex, our German Shepherd, didn't come to greet me. The house felt empty. I was trying to figure out what had happened when my next-door neighbor popped in. She said Rex had gotten loose and run out into the street. A truck hit him.

She called animal control. They decided he was dead and disposed of the remains."

"How did you respond?"

"I didn't know what to do. I was dumbfounded. At first, I was going to thank her, but then I thought, 'Who the hell are you to be doing that?' And I yelled, 'Was he even dead?'"

Tereza seemed to find that humorous. She smiled but didn't laugh.

"We went back and forth for a minute or two before she stormed out of the house in tears."

"Have you apologized to her?"

MacGregor glared at the gypsy. "No."

She smiled enigmatically. He continued, "My suspicion about the brain tumor proved correct. It was malignant. They gave me six months."

"Is that when you decided to undertake this Spirit Quest?"

"I'm not on a Spirit Quest," MacGregor bellowed. He stopped and calmed himself. "I'm going to meet my cousin before I die."

"That's the most important thing you have to do with your last six months on earth? What about your children?"

"They don't care about me. Haven't heard from them in years." He sipped his coffee. It was cold and nasty. "They're in my will. That's all that matters."

"You are normally intelligent and well organized," Tereza observed. "But in this case, you have abandoned everything and taken off on a quixotic cross-country trip."

"I got a second opinion. A specialist confirmed the diagnosis and prescribed some drugs to keep me functioning until the very end." MacGregor paused to glare at the gypsy. "I put my affairs in order. Then I took off."

"I see."

"I considered buying a gun and getting it over with. But that would have been messy. One night I remembered this cousin I had corresponded with from time to time. I decided I should hook up with her. While I was making plans, I decided to drive out there and see parts of the country I've never visited."

"Sounds like a Spirit Quest to me."

He waved in disgust. Tereza packed her things. She handed him a business card as she stood to leave. "Call me when you are ready to talk some more."

The woman was tall and burly. Her legs were wrapped in a sleek ankle-length black skirt. She paused to study him then took his face in her soft, warm hands and kissed his forehead. "I see great success for your undertaking. Eat your breakfast. You have a long journey ahead."

She scooped up her belongings and smiled at Mac one last time. "We will meet again before this is over."

Then she was gone.

2

MacGregor continued northwest along US Route 33. He passed through Columbus and stopped for a cup of coffee and a sandwich at a Quiki-Mart near Richmond, Indiana. He had covered 200 miles in three hours.

The cups and urns were at the back of the store. He grabbed a 12-ounce cup of black coffee and a ham sandwich before joining the end of a slow-moving checkout line.

There were still five customers in front of him when two men wearing ski masks charged in waving pistols. "Everybody back," one of them ordered. "All the way to the back. Move."

The other one pointed a pistol at the cashier and handed her a sack. "Empty the register."

People in front of Mac pushed into him as they backed away from the gunman. When he stepped back, he bumped into someone. He turned to look. It was a tall, rangy dude. The guy took a step back. Mac stepped into the spot he had vacated. The customers in front backed into him again. The man with the gun moved toward them, forcing the line of customers to the rear of the store.

There were five rows of shelving and six shopping aisles. The shelves were stocked with motor oil, school supplies, canned foods, chips, packaged breakfasts, and sandwiches for lunch. Mac had been looking down an aisle with doughnuts, cupcakes, and chips when the robbers burst into the store. As people backed away from the gun, the line lurched to the rear of the shopping area, working from the checkout counter past warming hot dogs, burritos, and ham and egg muffin sandwiches to the frozen goods section. The robber waved his gun, directing the line around the corner into the aisle with dairy products, microwaveable meals, ice cream, and bags of ice. Mac pushed the guy behind him all the way to the end of that row. They were a step away from an intersecting aisle that led to the front of the store.

There was a pause in the action. Fear set in as the customers waited for the next shoe to drop. The gangster pointed his gun ominously, his face and his thoughts hidden behind a ski mask. His partner escorted the clerk to the back. They were in no hurry.

Mac was torn between two impulses. On the one hand, he had read newspaper reports about robberies like this. They didn't end well. On the other hand, nothing serious had happened the last time an asshole pointed a gun at him. These guys might take what they wanted and leave if everyone stayed calm.

The clerk was marched to the left, where a doorway led to an unlit room. Minutes later, the robber came out without her and walked to the first man in line. He held out his sack. "Valuables."

The guy emptied his pockets and dropped a wristwatch into the bag. Then he was taken back to the darkened room to join the clerk. The gunman returned without him and approached the woman at the front of the line. She obediently deposited her purse and jewelry in the swag bag before being herded into the storage area.

Mac bumped against the guy behind him and whispered, "We've got to get out now."

"Yeah. But they've got a clean shot at the door."

"We could go through the window."

"How you gonna break the glass?"

"There are cases of drinks at the front. That might do it."

"Shut up," a gruff voice ordered.

They stopped talking. The guy with the sack came back out to collect his next victim. As the man began putting his things into the bag, Mac turned and shoved his accomplice. They bolted around the end of the shelves. Mac suddenly realized his partner was a kid. Probably still in high school. He was fast and quiet. Mac couldn't keep up. One of the gunmen yelled, "Hey."

He fired a shot, but shelves of merchandise covered the escape. The kid had reached the front of the store. He scooped up a 12-pack of colas, stepped past the last shelf, and fired the carton at the plate glass window. He threw it side-arm like a basketball pass.

A bullet buzzed past Mac's head. The storefront window shattered. Alarms went off. All hell broke loose.

The next shot hit Mac in the shoulder as he crossed an aisle. It spun him around. He fell back against a shelf full of cans and blacked out.

Mac sat for a moment looking around and reorienting himself. He remembered running. He did not remember falling. He was running and then he was on the floor. He had no idea how long he had been sitting there. That time was lost.

He rolled to his hands and knees so he could get back on his feet. He pulled his left leg up to his chest and set his foot on the floor. A hand grabbed his right bicep and pulled. Hot pain shot through his arm. He groaned, "Oh shit."

He looked up. A young woman in uniform was trying to help him stand. He pushed himself up with his left leg and dragged his right foot into position. He wobbled a little. The cop gripped his elbow to steady him. She was staring at his shoulder. Mac looked. There was a hole in his shirt and some blood. The cop said, "You've been shot."

He made a fist, flexed the muscles, and moved his arm up and down. The pain was excruciating. Mac scrunched his nose and shook his head. "It's nothing."

The officer kept her hand under his elbow as she led him out of the store. He counted three police cruisers in the parking lot. An ambulance had just parked. The EMT/driver was opening up the back for business. Mac was going to be her first customer.

The medic helped him out of his corduroy shirt and tee-shirt so she could examine the wound. A bullet had entered the side of his shoulder, bored a hole through the muscles, and exited. No bones, blood vessels, or nerves had been damaged. She treated the wound with antiseptic and sprayed a pain killer on his shoulder before bandaging it. She wanted to take him to lie down in the back of the ambulance so she could drive him to a hospital after she had seen the other victims. Mac refused. He promised to see a doctor as soon as he got to his cousin's house in St. Louis.

The woman wagged her head in disapproval. "Are you allergic to ampicillin?"

He growled, "I'm not allergic to anything."

"I'll be right back," she said as she climbed into the ambulance.

Mac studied the parking lot. He noticed the kid standing near the front of a police cruiser. Two cops had him hemmed in. It looked like they had cuffed him and were hassling him. He was stoic. Staring up at the sky. Mac started toward the group. "Hey. What's going on?"

"Stay back, Sir."

He kept walking toward them. "What's going on?"

"Stay back, Sir. This is police business."

"Are you arresting this man?"

"You need to stay back."

"On what grounds?"

One of them, sporting a PFC stripe on his left sleeve, turned to glare at the old man. Mac realized he looked pathetic. His alabaster torso hadn't seen the light of the sun in decades. Soft rolls of flesh had replaced rock-hard abs. His arms dangled at his side. He exercised just enough to maintain muscle tone. He wasn't going to intimidate anyone. Still, he was hot and feeling fierce. "I'll have your badges if you don't release him immediately."

For some reason, the cop responded, "We caught him fleeing the scene of the crime."

The PFC's patrol car had been sitting in traffic waiting for a light change when a case of soda flew through the front window of the Quiki-Mart. He and his partner observed a black man jump through the shattered glass and sprint across the parking lot. The cop riding shotgun jumped out to apprehend the man while the PFC maneuvered his cruiser into the lot. The cops paid no attention to the two men who raced from the store and burned rubber getting out of the parking lot.

Mac managed to keep a somewhat professional demeanor. Instead of 'fuck', he said, "He was going for help. We fled the scene because armed robbers were in the store getting ready to shoot us."

"He broke that window and tore off across the parking lot."

"Because I told him to."

The other cop demanded, "Who the hell are you?"

"Release this man immediately."

"We have him for destruction of property and fleeing the scene of a crime."

"You've got yourself a career-ending lawsuit. Racial profiling and other violations of his civil rights."

"You a lawyer?"

"A damn good one with connections. Let him go."

The PFC hesitated. Some on-lookers had pulled out cellphones and started recording. One of them stepped forward. "Ed Turner, Channel 5 News."

The cops clearly had a problem and needed a way out. Mac said, "Why don't you let him go before we have to sue for ten million or so?"

The PFC walked up to Mac. Turner joined the group. The cop ordered Turner to step back and turn off his recording. He turned to Mac. They stood toe-to-toe, but the cop had three or four inches and fifty pounds. He growled, "What's your version?"

"I was in line waiting to buy coffee and a sandwich when two guys with guns walked in and forced us to the back of the store. They lined us up against the freezers and started taking us one-by-one into a back room. The kid and I decided we had to get out of there, so we took off."

He studied Mac with a poker-faced stare. "Go on."

"You'll have to ask somebody else. I was running to the front. They were shooting. One of the bullets hit me and knocked me down. I couldn't see what was going on after that."

"Were you heading for the door or the window?"

"The window. They had a clean shot at the door."

The PFC crossed his arms and sneered, "How did you plan to get out the window?"

"The kid was going to break it."

"Can I see some identification?"

Mac pulled out a driver's license. The cop snapped a picture while Mac held it against his chest.

The cop glared at the old man for a long moment before turning and walking back to his partner. They removed the cuffs and retreated to the entrance of the convenience store. Turner reached the kid first. Mac pushed past him and pulled the young man aside. The teen was fuming. "Don't expect me to thank you for rescuing my black ass."

"I just wanted to thank you for getting us out of that store."

"I wouldn't have done it if you hadn't pushed me."

"The important thing is you did it."

"Yeah. And now I'm charged with a robbery."

"That won't stick. There are plenty of witnesses, and Turner will take your side on the news."

"What about you?"

"I have to get to St. Louis."

"You're the only witness who can back me up."

Mac looked at his feet. He owed this boy something. But there are hard truths in this life that you can't get around. He sucked in a breath and let it out. "What's your name?"

"Tim Johnson."

Mac held out his hand. They shook. "I'm Don MacGregor. I owe you. I might not be alive if it weren't for what you just did. But there's a tumor on my brain. It's killing me. I'll probably be dead and buried by the time this goes to trial."

The young man's eyes widened in shock. "I'm sorry, Sir."

"Don't be. Everybody dies. What counts is how you live."

They bumped fists. Mac said, "Take care."

The EMT was waiting at the ambulance. She gave Mac a pill and a cup of water. He swallowed them. She handed him four packages. "These will tide you over until you can get in to see a doctor. Take one packet every 12 hours."

"Can I go now?"

"Sit here. You took a bad fall. I want to make sure you're okay."

"I need to get something to eat." Mac pointed to his camper. "I'm going over there and see what's in the fridge."

The medic threw her arms up in frustration. "Okay, but come back here in 20 minutes so I can take another look at you."

Mac pulled on his clothes as he walked past the covey of police cars jammed into the small parking area. As soon as he was in his camper, he grabbed a Mountain Dew from his small refrigerator and a large bag of chips from a cabinet. It was not the meal he was hoping for, but it would have to do. He sat in the driver's seat and downed the soda while he watched the EMT examine the other victims. He checked his watch. It was four o'clock. He pulled out of the parking lot. It would take another 4 or 5 hours to reach St. Louis. He was pissed about the cup of coffee, but he wasn't going to chance another stop until he crossed the Mississippi.

3

MacGregor was doing well for an old man. He put in three hours before stopping for a pee break and a cup of coffee at a truck stop near Effingham, Illinois. He gassed up, parked the RV and went inside to take care of business. He came out with a bottle of extra-strength Tylenol and a hot apple turnover to go with his coffee.

He washed down the turnover and a couple of pills while he researched RV parks near St. Louis. A place just outside the city caught his attention. He called. A man with a hint of a drawl answered, "Camp Discovery. Eddie speaking."

"This is Don MacGregor. I need a place to park my camper tonight. I was hoping I could make a reservation with you."

"We have open sites. When do you expect to get here?"

"An hour or two. It looks like I've got a hundred miles to go but it's all freeway."

"It's late. Pick an empty spot when you get here. We can handle the paperwork in the morning." There was a pause. Then, "Can you find us?"

"I've got you on my GPS. Shouldn't have any trouble."

"Okay. See you in the morning."

"Eddie."

"Yeah."

"Is there somewhere nearby where I can get dinner?"

"Sam's Diner is open all night. Do you want directions?"

MacGregor punched the diner's name into his GPS and chuckled, "I found it. I'll be fine."

It was almost eight by the time he got back on the highway. He pulled into Sam's Diner after ten. A hundred miles on the interstate was no problem. Navigating the streets of a strange city at night was another matter. The place was deserted. A dozen empty booths lined the walls. Bar stools at the counter were unoccupied.

MacGregor took a seat in a booth near the door. A woman behind the counter looked up from her magazine. She gave him a couple of minutes and came over with a pot of coffee. "Do you know what you want? Or do you need some time?"

MacGregor looked up from the menu. "I'll take the cheeseburger."

The woman returned to her station and fired up the grill. She was waitress, cashier, and short-order cook on this shift. MacGregor looked around the joint while she prepared his meal. It reminded him of the places where he and the gang would hang out after a high school football game. It even had a jukebox that looked like it might work. Drab walls were covered with memorabilia – mostly school banners and photos of big-name athletes. One wall featured Cardinals' baseball greats. MacGregor recognized Stan Musial and Bob Gibson. The others he had never heard of.

The waitress set his meal on the table and placed a check beside it. She stood watching the old man. When he looked up, she said, "You don't look so good. Are you okay?"

He scrunched his nose and growled, "I'm fine."

She shrugged and went back to her magazine. MacGregor glanced over at her as he sipped his coffee. *Young enough to be my daughter. Granddaughter maybe. Long and lean. Dishwater blonde. No makeup. Carries herself like she's seen some tough times.*

He had overreacted. Probably fatigue from a very long day. The more he studied the woman, the more he felt compelled to make amends. "Can I buy you a cup of coffee?"

She looked up from her magazine, studied the old man, and returned to her reading.

"I'll throw in a piece of pie."

Nothing.

"I'll double your tip."

Still nothing.

"Look. I can't enjoy this meal with you sitting over there like that."

The counter-lady set her magazine down, took two pieces of apple pie from a dessert case on the counter, and poured a cup of coffee. MacGregor thought *That's exactly how Anne would do it. She had to let you know she was in charge.*

The woman brought the coffee, pie, and herself to his table. Her manner was stately, insolent.

She watched in silence while he ate. Then she pulled his plate out of the way and pushed a piece of pie to him. He nodded. "Thank you."

She picked up a fork and took a bite of her pie.

He asked, "You married?"

"No. You?"

"Used to be."

"What happened?"

"She died."

The woman shook her head. "I'm sorry."

"Not your fault. Could you tell me your name?"

"Katherine. What's yours?"

"Donald."

He studied her face as he chewed a bite of pie. *Beautiful green eyes.* He added, "MacGregor."

"What brings you here at this time of night, Mr. MacGregor?"

"There's an RV park a few miles up the road. I wanted to get some dinner before I called it a day."

"You look peaked. Are you okay?"

"I told you, I'm fine.'"

She ignored that. "You don't live around here. Where are you from?"

He sipped his coffee. "Maryland."

"That's a long drive."

"Took me all day."

Katherine took another bite of pie and sipped her coffee. "And where are you going?"

His eyes narrowed. It crossed his mind that she was building up to something. But he couldn't put his finger on it. She cocked her head and raised her eyebrows.

"I'm on my way to visit a cousin in Alaska."

She chewed another bite of pie. "That's another very long drive. You shouldn't be trying it alone."

Macgregor grimaced. He took a bite of pie and shook his head as he chewed. She chided, "You asked me to sit with you."

"You got a boyfriend?"

A wry smile. She shook her head.

"Why not?"

"Too busy. Not that it's any concern of yours."

He sat back and studied her. "Just trying to be conversational."

"I'm a nurse at an assisted living facility." She smirked. "That keeps me busy."

"And yet, you're working here at night."

"It's either that or sit home and do nothing." She grinned. "I get paid to sit here and do nothing."

MacGregor nodded sagely. He finished his coffee and got up to leave. "It was nice meeting you, Katherine."

"I'm a certified caregiver. You could use my help."

MacGregor snarled, "I don't need any help."

"You have serious medical issues, Mr. MacGregor. At some point, you are going to experience a medical emergency. Something you can't handle."

"Then I'll die. Big deal."

"What if you don't die?" Katherine paused. When the old man didn't respond, she continued. "You could be paralyzed for months or even years."

He froze. Intermediate outcomes hadn't crossed his mind. "I'll have to cross that bridge when I come to it."

"Even if you don't want to think about your own situation," Katherine admonished, "you should consider the other people you are putting at risk."

"Other people?"

"Other drivers. What if you have a medical emergency while you're barreling down the highway at 70 miles an hour? What is going to happen to the other drivers on the road?"

MacGregor shrugged. "Never had a problem like that."

"But you've never been in this situation."

"Wha'do you know about it?"

"I work with elderly patients in all stages of health, from robust to failing fast." She bit on her lower lip. "I don't know if you have weeks or months, but I am certain you have less time than you want to admit."

They stared at each other. MacGregor saw what she was up to, and he knew she had him where she wanted him. "What's in it for you?" He challenged.

"I've been treading water for years. I need a change of scenery."

"That's it?"

"I get room and board plus one hundred dollars a day."

He chuckled and shook his head. "Nah."

"That's cheap," she retorted. "For the time being, you can take care of yourself, but wouldn't it be nice to have someone take care of the cooking, cleaning, and shopping. And help with the driving." She lowered her head and rolled her eyes up to look at him. "Down the road, you may need someone to wait on you hand and foot."

MacGregor turned and looked up at the ceiling. "Shit."

"You know what's coming," Katherine said. "You know I'm right."

He started to walk away. He turned back because he couldn't shake the image of a multicar pileup on an interstate. "You ready to go?"

"I need a day to take care of things and pack. I can leave tomorrow afternoon."

"I have to be out of the RV park by noon."

"Tell Eddie you're waiting for me. He'll let you stay until I get there."

MacGregor stared at her. *Are you serious?*

"We're friends. We've dated from time to time." She stood to shake his hand. "The last thing I'll have to do is drop my car off with my cousin and have you sign the contract he'll draw up." She took MacGregor's hand and held on. "Maybe you should plan on spending an extra night so we can start off early the day after tomorrow."

On a sudden whim, he pulled her hand to his lips and kissed it. "As you wish."

4

———

Mac woke to the sound of banging on the camper's door. He opened his eyes and pushed up on his elbows. Pain shot through his right shoulder. His head fell back to the pillow. The rapping started again. He yelled, "I'm on my way."

The knocking stopped. He pushed up with his left arm and pulled his legs over the edge of the bed. *Who the hell is that? It's too early for that damned waitress.*

He looked down at his tee-shirt and boxers. That should be enough. He stood. Wobbled. Steadied himself with his left hand. And plodded barefoot to the door.

A swarthy visitor, his hair cut short military-style, grinned up at Mac. He radiated an infectious friendliness. "Hi. I'm Eddie. I just came by to make sure you were okay."

Mac looked up. The sun was directly overhead. *Noon. Shit.* He shook his head in disgust. "I'm fine." He ran his fingers through what was left of his hair. "Fifteen hours on the road must have taken more out of me than I expected."

"Come on over to the office when you're ready, and we can take care of the paperwork."

"Give me five minutes." Mac pressed his lips together in a tight-lipped smile. "My plans have changed. I've decided to stay tonight and leave early tomorrow morning."

Eddie nodded. "No problem." He started to leave, stopped, and turned back. "I'm getting ready to make burritos. You're welcome to join me."

"Sounds good," Mac wheezed. "See you in five."

It took the old man more like 20 minutes to reach the back door of the rental office. The smell of spices cooking with meat and cheese in a skillet wafted through the screen. He rapped on the wooden frame. Eddie yelled, "It's open. C'mon in."

Mac stepped into the kitchen and stood adjusting to the dim light. The younger man was at the stove working burrito ingredients with a spatula. He was the same height as Mac but easily twenty pounds heavier. Muscles rippled under the tee-shirt that hung loosely over his torso and down over the top of his jeans. His brown suede jungle mocs looked like they had seen a lot of miles.

"I apologize for dragging you out of bed, Mr. MacGregor," Eddie said as he turned to flash a grin. "I know you got in late but I couldn't wait any longer."

"That's okay. Call me Don. I'm not much for formalities."

"Did you get enough rest?"

"Yeah. I got nuthin' goin' on today. I can take a nap if I need it."

Eddie began loading up tortillas with refried beans and burrito mix. "Where are you headed?"

"Alaska."

"You've got a long drive. Where'd you start?"

Mac watched Eddie fold and wrap the tortillas around the meat and cheese. It took a minute to realize the young man performed this feat with only one hand. His right arm hung at his side. Mac broke the spell and said, "Annapolis."

Eddie finished up the wraps. "Where in Alaska?"

"I have a cousin in Fairbanks."

"Nice place. I visited it on a weekend pass when we were training in the Yukon."

Eddie split the burritos onto two plates. He picked up one with his left hand and passed it to his right. He grabbed the other one and brought both plates to the kitchen table. Mac asked, "When was that?"

Eddie handed him a plate and set the other on the table in front of his own chair. "Eight years ago, before we deployed to Afghanistan."

Mac set his plate down and took a seat. Eddie asked, "Do you want something to drink? I have coffee and water. No beer. I don't drink."

"Coffee's fine."

Eddie went out to the front office and returned with Mac's coffee. "I guess you'll be heading north. That's the shortest route."

"I've decided to follow the Lewis and Clark Trail. I'm in no hurry."

Eddie liked that idea. He began rattling off highlights from his own trip along the trail. Mac interrupted to ask about the right arm. The young man shrugged. "It's not completely useless. I can raise it waist high, and I can carry things."

The injury was bad enough to get him a medical discharge and disability payments.

"How'd it happen?"

"The lieutenant decided to take a side trip. We drove into an ambush."

"That happened once in Nam."

"How bad?"

"No casualties. We hit the gas and bugged out."

"We got caught in a firefight. It lasted over an hour."

"And you were wounded."

"Yeah. I took a couple of rounds."

Eddie's father brought the family from Guatemala in the sixties. He had taught biology in college before retiring to a small ranch in Texas. Eddie was the youngest of seven kids. He had joined the Army right out of high school and eventually made it into the Special Forces.

An alarm from a cell phone interrupted the discussion. Someone was calling Flores' Towing Service for roadside assistance. That was the vet's other business. It provided a steady income without being too demanding, except when somebody needed immediate help. Eddie put the call on speaker so he could jot down the caller's name, location, and credit card number. He had to rescue the stranded motorist immediately, but before he took off, he handed Mac some papers to fill out.

The old man finished his breakfast and completed the rental agreement. He cleared the dishes from the table and left them soaking in the sink. Then he took the paperwork out to the front desk.

As he left the kitchen, he passed a hallway leading to another part of the building. A bedroom or two and a bathroom with a tub and shower would be at the far end. The Camp Discovery office occupied the living room of the century-old cottage.

Mac left by the front door. It closed and locked on its own. He checked. A sign next to the door gave instructions for getting a camping slot and registering when the owner was out of the office.

His injured shoulder throbbed. It felt like it had been hit with a baseball bat instead of a slug no bigger than a man's thumb. He needed more Tylenol. The deal with Katherine was starting to bother him. He was having second thoughts about bringing her along. The problems were obvious in the clear light of day. If it weren't for her, he'd be on his way to Alaska. But they had an agreement, so he had to sit around waiting for her to show up.

As he walked back to the camper, he noticed a swimming pool with a concession stand. Two teenagers were playing cards at a table on the deck beside the pool. Memories came unbidden.

His mother hated going in the water. She couldn't swim. But she was determined her kids would be able to. She took them to lessons at the YMCA. Mac wandered to the edge of the pool and stood entranced. In his mind, he watched his sister swim the length of the pool. She was smooth and effortless from the first time she tried. His first attempt was nearly a disaster. He had jumped in and immediately started thrashing. The instructors had to pull him out before he drowned. Standing at the edge of this pool, Mac could taste the water rushing into his mouth and feel the panic as if it had happened yesterday.

He continued his trek to the camper. Better memories popped up. Both he and his sister passed the Red Cross Life Saving exam. Both qualified as lifeguards. Neither managed to get a job. He was on the swim team in high school. She wasn't. They probably didn't even have a girls' swim team back then.

Mac made the team because he could gut it out to finish longer races like the 200 fly. It was the same in track. He ran the mile and two-mile. He won some races but only because the competition wasn't very good.

That was his life in a nutshell. Good at everything but never *that* good. He took after his parents. Intelligent and hard-working. His mother grew up on a farm and moved to the city. She raised a family and taught school. His father dropped out of high school and found a job at the shipyard. He worked his way up to middle management before calling it quits.

They played by the rules. Did the right thing. That's a good formula but it won't get you to the top.

Mac had a sudden urge to put all this in writing. He took out his laptop and started typing. Not that anybody would be interested. He needed to preserve his past because he hadn't asked enough questions about his parents. Now they were gone. Wishing he had gotten their story didn't help.

He gave up after a couple of pages and stretched out on the couch for a nap.

5

anging on the camper's door brought Mac out of a sound sleep. He opened the door to find Katherine standing outside. Blue cotton blouse over a white tee shirt. Loose-fitting white shorts. Slip-on loafers. No socks. "I finished sooner than expected, so I came early." She smiled sheepishly. "I hope that's okay."

He held the door open. "Come on in."

"Did I wake you?"

"Yeah," he grumbled.

"Sorry. I didn't want to keep you waiting any longer than necessary."

She carried a suitcase up the steps and looked around. There wasn't much to see in what amounted to a tricked-out walk-in closet. The cockpit with swivel chairs for the driver and a passenger was on her right. She stood next to the sink with its tiny landing area. Cabinet space above and below. A toaster oven and a microwave were stacked next to the sink. On the other side of the microwave, a TV was mounted over a small refrigerator. A clever sofa that could seat four side-by-side or fold around into two seats that faced each other took up most of the opposite wall. A table was attached to the base of the sofa. A Murphy bed large enough to fill most of the living space was stowed against the wall above it. Dressers and a wardrobe were attached to the wall between the kitchenette and the shower at the far end of the cabin. The bathroom was across from the shower.

MacGregor followed her gaze. She paused to study the bed, and he realized sleeping arrangements would be a problem. "I didn't plan on a roommate when I bought this thing."

She shrugged. "I don't see why it won't work."

"It sleeps two, but there's only one bed."

She cocked her head, lips curled up on one side. "I have a sleeping bag in the car."

He pointed to her suitcase. "Is that all you're bringing? Most women need three or four."

A glare flashed across her face. "I have another one in the car if you have room for it."

"I'll get it," he offered with obligatory gallantry.

"First rule, Mr. MacGregor: I take care of myself. I'll bring the other one aboard later if there's still room."

"Stop calling me 'Mr.'," he snapped. "Call me Don or Mac or even MacGregor, but I hate 'Mr. MacGregor.'"

She extended her hand. "Kate."

When he reached out, pain shot through his arm. He saw stars. A soft "wow" escaped.

"What's wrong?"

"My shoulder. Hurt it yesterday. No big deal."

She held his right hand while her left hand worked up his arm, searching for the pain. "What happened?"

"I was shot."

"And that's not a big deal?"

"It's just a scratch."

"Let me see. Has it been treated?"

"The ambulance lady bandaged it and gave me some ampicillin."

"How much?"

"Four packets."

Her lips tightened into a line. "That's not enough. Do you have a prescription for more?"

He shook his head.

"You need to see a doctor." Kate sighed. "I can get you in first thing in the morning." She took a step back. "Take your shirt off and let me have a look."

The bandage was bloody. Kate probed his shoulder with her fingertips. "I don't suppose the EMT flushed that wound."

He shook his head.

"I want to get you to a doctor now."

"What about your cousin?"

"He can wait."

She held out her hand as Mac pulled his shirt on. "Why don't you give me the keys? It'll be easier if I drive."

Fifteen minutes later, they pulled up to the clinic at the back of St. Elizabeth's Senior Living Facility. Inside, a few people sat along the wall or in wheelchairs waiting for attention. Mac followed Kate across the lobby. When they reached the reception desk, the large woman in a pink uniform said, "I thought you were gone."

She hadn't looked up from her magazine. Kate barked, "Mr. MacGregor needs medical attention."

"What's the problem?"

"Gunshot wound."

"We can't treat that."

"It's minor," Kate countered. "The bandage has to be replaced. He needs a prescription for Ampicillin. Could you please get someone to look at him?"

The administrative aide looked up to study Mac. "Keesha Jones" was embossed on her name tag. She asked, "Does he have insurance?"

Kate turned to Mac. He stared back at her. "Do you have insurance, Mac?"

He thought for a moment. Cleared his throat and said, "Medicare. I'm on Medicare."

Jones handed a clipboard to Kate. "Take him to Number Three. Fill out these forms while you're waiting."

The small exam room was crowded with furniture. A computer sat on a tray at the end of a rotating arm with an attached stool. It was pushed against the wall. A small sink and a chest containing medical supplies took up one corner. A couple of chairs had been placed against the back wall. A large recliner took up the middle of the room. It could be rotated horizontally and vertically. The hydraulic lift it rested on could raise and lower it as needed. The back was positioned halfway up like a raised bed. Kate had Mac sit on it and complete the questionnaire. She sat on one of the chairs against the back wall.

Mac ran through the list of questions checking off 'No' for all the ailments. That took no more than five minutes. Kate asked to see his answers. "You my doctor?"

"No."

"I'll wait for the doctor. No need going through it twice."

"High blood pressure?"

"Nope."

"Diabetes?"

"I'm okay. I've got some problems but medicine's not going to fix them."

She rolled her eyes but let it go. They waited. After another ten minutes, which seemed like an eternity, a stout, gray-haired woman walked in and introduced herself as Dr. Gert Williams. She sent Kate back to the lobby before turning her attention to Mac.

"So, you are in perfect health, Mr. MacGregor?"

"All things considered."

"For instance?"

"I'm an old man, and I'm not getting any younger."

"What is your blood pressure – typically?"

"100 to 110."

"When was the last time you had it checked?"

"Six months or so. But I was monitoring it daily."

"Are you on any medication for blood pressure?"

"Yeah. A little pink pill."

"Lisinopril?"

"Sounds right."

"How much?"

"Five milligrams."

"How about diabetes? What's your A1C?"

Mac eyed Williams suspiciously. He considered feigning ignorance but that would give her an excuse to order a blood test. He mumbled, "7.2."

"Are you on any medication?"

"The doctor said I'd be okay without it."

"I see," she sighed. "How did you get that scar on the side of your head?"

Mac tried to maintain a poker face while he considered his answer. In the end, he muttered, "They removed a tumor."

"Was it malignant?"

"Stage four."

"What is your treatment protocol?"

"Don't have one. I tried radiation and chemo and decided I'd rather be dead."

Dr. Williams chuckled. "I would be failing you as a patient if I simply bandaged your wound and gave you antibiotics. You need treatment for the glioblastoma. I have to be concerned about interactions among the medications you will be taking."

"I tried that. Chemo doesn't work for me. Radiation sounds backward. You're going to hit me with a dose of X-rays that would cause cancer if I didn't already have it. Surgery to remove a tumor is risky. And it doesn't cure anything."

She nodded. "A good summary, but I would say that the surgery buys time for the chemotherapy to kill the cancer."

"I notice you didn't say anything about curing it. Can you cure the cancer?"

"No. But we can give you a longer life with less suffering."

"Chemo inflicts its own suffering. I wouldn't be able to function at all if I had to deal with chemo and radiation." Mac glared at the doctor, waiting for her reaction. She watched him with a faint smile that revealed nothing. He snorted and continued, "I went over this with my oncologist before I told him to shove it. He gave me a ninety-day supply of some experimental drug and a prescription for pain pills. I'm supposed to go back and see him in sixty to ninety days."

"What did he give you?"

"Don't know and don't care."

Mac pulled a small package of prescriptions from his wallet and handed it to Williams. She found the cancer meds and checked them on her computer. "He has you on chemotherapy," she said. "The medication he gave you is designed to administer the cancer-fighting cocktail in small, frequent doses. That's easier on your system. We would take a similar approach. But we would do more than hand you marketing samples of an experimental drug and wish you good luck."

"I like his approach."

"Who is your regular physician? Is he or she aware of the medication Dr. Evans gave you?"

"Jacobs. Barry Jacobs. I imagine he is. The two of them were working together."

Williams wasn't happy, but Mac was ready to walk out with an injury that could develop a fatal infection rather than submit to cancer treatments. She cleaned the bullet wound and applied a fresh bandage.

6

When Dr. Williams had finished with Mac, she brought Kate back into the exam room and made her sit where she could see the old man's chart on the computer screen. The doctor stood next to the door with her arms folded across her chest. Her eyes went from Kate to Mac and back as she appraised them. After a minute or two, she gave her summary of his condition. They listened stoically until she got to the stage four glioblastoma. Williams said, "I believe you are making a mistake. But your minds are made up. I wish you the best."

Kate stood and gave Mac a withering look. She walked over and embraced her friend. The doctor held her for a minute before letting go.

Kate walked out of the exam room and out of the clinic on autopilot. She marched to the camper, head down, deep in thought. Mac's diagnosis and Dr. Williams' instructions were disturbing. Mac's scar hadn't registered when they were eating dinner and negotiating their agreement. That bothered her. She told herself it was because the old man looked dead on his feet. He had been exhausted from driving all day. And, she now realized, trauma and blood loss from the gunshot wound had made his situation far worse. Add brain cancer. She was looking at a nightmare scenario.

War raged in her mind blocking out the world around her. Litigators argued the situation. On her left, her mother shouted angrily, "You can't move in with that man. He'll destroy you."

On her right, a maniacal Jack Nicholson chided, "C'mon. You got nothin'. You gotta get on that bus and get outta here while you can."

Her mother, fit to be tied, screamed, "He'll kill you. If he doesn't, he'll leave you high and dry."

Nicholson cackled. He leaned into her with a wide-eyed grin. "Last chance to live. You got nothin' to lose. The old bat's afraid yer gonna be happy."

He was right. Her mom was right. She should tell Mac she couldn't do it. But he would go on without her. And when there was a pile-up on an interstate because he had a stroke, it would be her fault.

Suddenly Mac was standing next to her with his hand out. "I'll drive."

Kate looked up. He glowered. She blushed. "Sorry." She retrieved the keys from her purse and handed them over. Mac opened the door and held it for her. When they were settled, she asked, "Can we go to Sam's for dinner?"

He started the engine. "I guess so. Why?"

"We don't have to."

Mac grimaced. "I just asked why."

"I want to say goodbye before I leave town. Sam's like a father to me."

Mac pulled up Sam's Diner as his destination. As soon as directions appeared on the GPS screen, he put the vehicle in gear and started rolling. "That doctor had a lot to say to you."

"What we are getting ready to do is risky. She would prefer to keep you in a facility where you could be cared for if something happens."

"You said you're a certified caregiver," Mac objected. "Can't you take care of me?"

"Yes. But I won't have all the resources I would have at St. Elizabeth's."

"Humph."

It was still early when Mac and Kate entered Sam's. The diner seemed more open and welcoming in the afternoon light. A few customers were seated at the counter. Two couples were eating dinner in the booths. Kate led the way to an empty booth.

A slender, balding man in a short-sleeved white shirt caught up with them as they reached their table. Kate paused to greet him. He kissed her on the cheek. "Thank you for coming to say goodbye."

He gave Mac a quick once-over. "So, this is your young man."

She scowled. "Mac, my boss, Sam Reinhart. He owns this establishment."

"Hi."

"Sam, this is Donald MacGregor, my new client. We are going to explore America and visit his cousin in Alaska."

Sam gestured for them to be seated. "May I join you for dinner?"

Mac looked at Kate. She looked at him. He turned to Sam and growled, "Sure. That would be nice."

A waitress had arrived and was standing by to take their order. Sam told her their meal would be on the house. He smiled at his guests. "Go ahead and get started. I will be with you in a few minutes."

When Sam returned with a bottle of kosher red wine and three glasses, Mac and Kate were eating in silence. He slid into the booth next to Kate and said, "So, Mr. MacGregor, what brings you to St. Louis?"

The old man pressed his lips into a line. "A getaway. I've decided to see the country."

"All alone?"

Mac rocked his head. "Kids have moved on. Wife's dead."

"I'm sorry. When?"

"Six months ago. How about you? You married?"

"Like you, I am without the love of my life."

Once Sam got going, he kept talking. His children had all graduated from college and started their own families. He used to own restaurants in Philadelphia and Washington DC. He sold them after his wife died. When he got tired of being home alone, he opened this place. It gave him a new lease on life.

Around nine, Kate patted Sam on the thigh. "We have to get back to the camper." She followed him as he got out of the booth. "Mac needs to get some rest, and I don't want you staying up too late."

She gave him a peck on the cheek. He hugged her. "Come back and see me."

Kate frowned. "What did you tell me about the future?"

"Today is all we have."

"So, no promises." She hugged him. "Except, I will never forget you and all that you have done for me."

A sad smile played across Sam's face. He took Mac's hand and pulled him in for a hug. "It was good to meet you. To sit and share with a gentleman like you. May Yahweh hold you in the palm of his hand always."

With that, he went back to work, and his guests left for their mobile home.

Mac fumed all the way to the camper. He glared out at the road while he jammed the latch plate of his seat belt into the buckle. "I don't appreciate being marched off to bed."

Kate kept her eyes straight ahead, suppressing a smile. "You were struggling to stay awake."

He started the engine. "I'm fine. I'm wide awake."

He backed out into the street. She looked at him out of the corner of one eye. A skeptical smile had won the battle. "The walk back from the diner revived you."

Mac shifted into drive and headed back to Camp Discovery. They rode in silence.

As soon as they were parked, Kate set up the bed and rolled out her sleeping bag next to the wall. She slipped off her blouse and shorts. Mac said, "I'm going to get a drink. Do you want one?"

He started toward the back for his whiskey. She blocked the aisle. "You've had a couple of glasses of wine. That's enough alcohol for one day."

"I'm getting a drink."

They stared at each other. Jaws set. Finally, she said, "Go sit down. I'll pour."

A few minutes later, Kate brought two cups to the front. Mac took the one from her right hand. She sat in the passenger's seat and held out her cup. "To a successful journey."

The cups clicked. "A successful journey."

7

Mac woke around two. Kate was next to him in her sleeping bag. He got up, peed, and rolled back into bed. She turned to look at him. "You okay?"

"Yeah."

He woke again at 4. Kate was still lying there. At six-thirty, she was up, stretching her lean body into yoga postures that stressed and highlighted toned muscles. A tank top and panties hid little. When she finished, she made her way back to the shower offering a cheery "Good morning" as she passed the bed.

Suddenly, the idea of driving across the country with a woman he had just met felt very strange. Mac had moved into the camper a week before starting the trip but only to sleep and shower. Now he was sharing it with a person he knew nothing about.

Kate stepped from the shower to the bathroom. She emerged fully dressed and asked, "What do you want for breakfast?"

"Eggs. Over easy. And toast. And coffee."

She nodded. "How about you get up and stow the bed while I get myself oriented."

Mac was dressing when Kate sang out, "You don't have any eggs. I found some Cheerios."

"Okay. I'll have Cheerios."

"Do you want to go to Sam's for a hot breakfast?"

If he had been alone, Mac would have poured a bowl of cereal and been done with it. But the eggs sounded better. "Okay."

"Did you pay Eddie?"

"No. He took off on a call. Then you took me to the doctor. Then we went to dinner."

"Let's go take care of that."

They found Eddie working his daily chores. He insisted they join him for breakfast. The Lewis and Clark Trail was the main topic of discussion. Eddie told Kate, "You should leave your car with me. I've got room in the garage and I'll make sure it's driven. You don't want it sitting idle all that time."

Back at the camper, Mac helped Kate move her stuff in. A quick inspection showed Mac was occupying the lion's share of the space. Three pairs of jeans, five heavy cotton work shirts, a pair of dress slacks, two no-iron blue pinstripe cotton shirts Anne had bought, a wine-red sport coat, and a leather jacket took up over half of the wardrobe.

His tee-shirts and boxer briefs occupied one drawer in the left-side dresser. Socks had another drawer. Sweaters and a sweatshirt were stowed in a drawer in the right-side dresser.

Mac was using both half-drawers in the top slot of the left-side dresser. Miscellany including nail clippers, electric razor, and chargers for his phone and laptop in one. Important papers in the other.

He had to consolidate. He could have one half-drawer. Underwear and socks would share one drawer. Sweaters, the sweatshirt, and the pinstripe dress shirts would get a second drawer. Pants could share hangers with shirts.

Kate went to get her other suitcase while Mac rearranged his clothes. On her way to the car, she called her cousin Jimmy to talk about the situation and figure out what legal documents would be needed. They agreed to get together in his office at one.

Her wardrobe was summery and practical. A dozen blouses. A dozen pairs of shorts. A dozen tank tops. She could go the whole trip without wearing the same outfit twice. She had flip-flops to supplement her canvas slip-on loafers. Her undies – cotton hipster panties – took up most of a drawer leaving just enough room for socks, stockings, and a couple of bras. She brought along three sets of slacks and blouse separates and a magenta blazer that would go with any of the outfits. Two pairs of heels and a black cocktail dress completed her wardrobe. She had packed a zippered cotton parka for cold mornings.

Kate had a necessities bag for make-up, lotions, perfume, pads, and other things, including band-aids, peroxide, and anti-bacterial ointment. She stowed that bag on the floor of the wardrobe.

The clothes they were leaving behind were packed in her suitcases. They were stashed in the trunk of her car. It was moved to the garage next to the rental office.

Kate's second cousin Jimmy - James E Graham III - ran a small law practice out of an old two-story frame house.

As soon as Kate led Mac into the reception area, Jimmy's assistant Aggie Lane came over for a hug. Then demanded, "What are you doing here?"

Kate sputtered, "We've got an appointment."

"Not according to my calendar."

"I talked to Jimmy this morning. He probably forgot to tell you."

Aggie grimaced. Her boss depended on her to manage the schedule and remind him of appointments. But he would forget to tell her when he decided to squeeze a client in. She led the pair back to his office, a repurposed dining room.

When Mac stepped into the room, his eyes came to rest on a large oak table. It was bare except for a keyboard and monitor and three manilla folders laid out neatly in front of the lawyer. "Whoa. I thought I was coming over to sign an agreement on terms of employment."

"You are, but a few additional issues must be addressed because of your situation."

"I have a verbal agreement with Kate. She will come along with me and perform housekeeping duties for $100 a day plus room and board."

Jimmy shot a look at Kate. "Do you have any health issues, Mr. MacGregor?"

"I'm getting older, but nothing significant."

"What about stroke? Are you at risk?"

"Insignificant. There's no history of stroke or heart attack in my family."

"But you've had brain surgery," the lawyer objected. "I can see the scar."

"If that's a problem," Mac snapped, "we can stop right now."

Kate put a hand on his arm. "Don't be like that, Mac," she soothed. "I don't have a problem. I wouldn't have gone to the trouble of making arrangements if I did."

"If you don't have a problem, why are you and your lawyer making a big production out of this?"

Kate took his hand and stepped around to face him. "We have to be upfront about the risks. You've had a tumor surgically removed. It was malignant, and you are refusing treatment. The tumor is going to grow back. That puts you at risk."

"I'm not going to waste my time and money on those treatments. They just prolong the agony."

"I know. I've watched people I cared deeply about go through it from start to finish." She brushed a hand across his face and head, letting her fingers linger on the scar. "I hope that if and when I'm in that situation, I'll have the courage to say 'Fuck it. I'm going to live until I die.'"

Her laser green eyes held the old man. He couldn't turn away. Tears welled up. He mumbled, "I don't know what I'm supposed to do."

"Yes, you do," she corrected. "You're doing it. But you have to think about the consequences for others."

Kate led Mac to a seat across from her cousin. He stared at the manilla folders before turning his gaze on the lawyer. "The symptoms were mild, but they never cleared up. An MRI revealed a tumor on the right side of my brain. The doctors operated. They removed a stage two tumor wrapped around a stage four glioblastoma."

Mac stood and walked around the room. It was organized chaos. The lawyer had a pile of paperwork on each of several chairs that sat against the wall. A stand at the back of the room had an aluminum pitcher and some Styrofoam cups. Whatever the pitcher held had reached room temperature. Either cold coffee or warm water. He turned to look at Jimmy. "I consulted with a couple of doctors and decided to pass on chemo and radiation." Mac grimaced and shook his head. "That left me stranded. A widower with no job. I wasn't ready to die, but I had nothing to live for." He wandered back to his seat. "My solution was this trip. See the country and meet face-to-face with a cousin I barely knew."

"Which brings us to the business at hand," Jimmy said. "We have to document that these are choices you've made of your own free will. We also need you to acknowledge that Katherine is not a doctor and cannot be expected to provide medical care while she is with you."

Mac bowed and shook his head slowly. He was beaten. There was no way around it. He raised up to meet the lawyer's gaze. "Understood."

"I will give you the benefit of my training and experience," Kate said. "You will have to see a physician any time you want official medical advice. I will do my best to get you in to see a doctor if that becomes necessary."

"CYA lawyer language. If I want real medical care, it's up to me to get it."

"Correct," Jimmy said. "Katherine is asking for power of attorney and the right to make medical decisions for you in the event that you become incapacitated."

"I'll make my own decisions."

"As long as you are capable. But you can become incapacitated. Doctors could even decide that you are not able to make sound decisions. In either case, somebody will make decisions for you. If you don't designate Katherine, you will be putting yourself in the hands of strangers."

Mac's head sank into his hands. *How did I get into this mess?* He took a deep breath and sighed. Kate squeezed his hand. She said softly, "It's going to be okay, Mac."

He looked up. She was smiling. "I understand this is difficult, but now is the time to address these issues. This is your chance to make your wishes known and put them in writing."

He nodded. "Okay. Kate gets power of attorney and the power to make medical decisions on my behalf if things get to the point that I can't make them myself."

"Do you have living relatives? I think this would be a good time to draw up a will."

"I've got a will. It's in the camper."

"Okay. Would you mind letting me make two copies? One for my records and one for Katherine."

"Now?"

"This would be a good time. We could use a break."

Walking out to the RV gave Mac time to think. *They're right about covering the bases before something happens. But that kind of thinking kills adventures. Kate led me into an ambush. What kind of game is she playing? Can I trust her if she needs all this CYA shit? Or is she just going along with it to satisfy her lawyer?*

When he got back, Mac handed the will to Jimmy and turned to Kate. "I need an honest answer. Can I trust you? Are you going to have my back? Or should I write this off as a bad idea and go ahead without you?"

Kate turned to face him. Her gaze pierced right through to his soul. "I'm with you, Mac. I'm excited about this trip. I don't like this BS any more than you, but I have to think about what might happen. If something goes wrong, I'll be the one on the hot seat. Not you."

That didn't help. It made a bad situation sound terrible. But he liked Kate. She would at least give him some company and brighten up the RV. At the same time, he couldn't stop thinking: *There's no fool like an old fool.*

As they were leaving, Jimmy told them about a rest stop not far up the road where they could park and sit as long as they wanted.

8

Jimmy's rest stop was the parking lot of a historic church at the top of Charbonier Bluff.

The lot was empty. Mac parked in front of the partially restored building. It was the main attraction. An old church that had been built on an Indian burial ground. The rest of the site looked like a small farm with wood frame buildings and a barn.

Kate insisted on getting out and walking around. Somewhere between the camper and the pathway leading up to the old church, Mac halted. He closed his eyes and tottered. The episode started with light-headedness. His arms went numb. Thighs. Knees threatened to buckle. He bent over and put his hands on his knees to steady himself. He forced himself to take long, deep breaths and let them out slowly.

Kate sensing something was wrong spun around and saw the old man struggling. In a panic, she reached out to steady him. "Are you okay?"

He straightened as feeling returned to his limbs. "Yeah. Blood pressure. It comes and goes."

She winced and pulled her chin in. Her lips formed a line that turned up at the edges. "Blood pressure?"

"I get a little light-headed like you get from low blood pressure when you stand up."

"You've been on your feet for a couple of minutes. Is there anything else?"

"My legs feel weak, and I get a funny sensation in my chest and shoulders."

"Sounds like tachycardia to me."

"What's that? Never heard of it."

"Your heart starts beating too fast for the blood supply so your body shuts down until your heart gets back in synch."

Mac shrugged. "Whatever. It's not worth worrying about."

"It's a serious medical condition. There are drugs to control it."

"Don't need 'em. It goes away by itself."

"It's likely to get worse."

He tapped the scar on his head. "Not in my case."

She closed her eyes and shook her head. Mac led the way to the ruins, Kate walked at his side lightly gripping his elbow. A display on the lawn next to the walkway that led to the museum entrance gave a brief history of the site.

Indians occupied the vantage point intermittently for centuries before European settlers arrived. According to legend it had been an Indian burial ground at one passed time. That gave rise to tales of visitors encountering Indian spirits.

Captain William Clark of the Lewis and Clark expedition climbed the hill on May 16, 1804, shortly after leaving St. Louis on the journey up the Missouri River. Clark noted in his diary that he could see St. Charles seven miles away.

Jesuit missionaries built a church in 1823. By the time they shut its doors in 1971, the compound had become the longest continuously operated Jesuit novitiate in the United States. The Missouri Department of Conservation took over the site in 1973.

On their way back to the RV, Kate asked, "Where to now?"

"I haven't thought that far ahead. I'll have to check my book."

The book was a tour guide to the Lewis and Clark Trail with a suggested itinerary for a two-week trip to the Oregon coast. Mac found Charbonier Bluff. "It looks like Jefferson City, Arrow Rocks, and Fort Osage are next."

Kate pulled up Google Maps on her tablet. "You won't be able to fit all that in today."

"Really?"

"Jefferson City is about 150 miles. Do you want to take the Interstate or the scenic route?"

"What's the difference?"

"Lewis and Clark took the scenic route. The Interstate is faster."

Driving to Jefferson City for an early start in the morning was the logical choice. Mac could see that, but it irked him. He felt cheated. "We can take the scenic route."

"Might as well enjoy the ride."

Kate made reservations at a campsite a few miles west of the city. "We should eat before we take off. It's not a good idea to eat just before bed."

"I'm not hungry and it's already late."

"So? We're going to spend the night." Kate waited for a response. Mac looked annoyed but said nothing. She went on, "You should relax. I'll drive."

Mac was hungrier than he wanted to admit. Sandwiches served with hot coffee hit the spot. They set off on a tree-lined rural road that wound through the hilly countryside more or less paralleling the river. The ride lulled Mac to sleep. Kate was going to let him doze, but the guards at the park entrance insisted on getting a credit card to cover the cost of their stay.

Mac woke at three. On the way to the bathroom, thoughts of Anne pushed into his consciousness. He was pissed at her for dying and leaving him alone. Harsh words raged in his mind. The feelings wouldn't let go. He poured some whiskey and sat in the captain's chair to calm down. By the time he found the Big Dipper and the North Star, the storm had passed. He was still nursing his scotch and studying the stars when Kate's hand on his shoulder broke the spell. "You okay?"

"Yeah. Just an old man living in the past."

"What about the past?"

He took another sip from his cup. She sat in the other chair. "What's the problem, Mac?"

He blew out through his lips. "Anne."

"Your wife?"

He nodded. Kate gently pulled the cup from his hand and took a swig. She passed it back. "How long has it been?"

"Six months."

"Did you find out about the cancer before or after?"

"After. I had been having headaches and vision problems. That's why I went to the doctor." He shook his head. "She got sick and died. It was very quick – less than a week. I didn't get back to my doctor until after the funeral."

"And you've been dealing with a double whammy ever since."

"Triple. Our dog was killed while I was with the doctor getting the bad news."

She snarfed. "I know that's not funny. But compared to the other two."

"That's why it's called the straw that broke the camel's back."

After a couple of minutes, she said, "You should write your story down."

"Nobody'd be interested."

"That's not the point. It's trying to get out. You're holding it in. Let it out, and it'll let go of you."

"I can't just write things for the heck of writing. I need to believe that somebody is interested in what I'm trying to say."

"There are websites for that. You'd meet people who are reaching out with their stories. They would love to hear yours."

You're serious. Flashed through Mac's brain. He said, "I don't know. Why don't you go back to bed? I'll be there as soon as I finish this."

Kate stood and kissed him on the cheek. "Don't be too long. You need your sleep."

9

The next time Mac woke, the sun had begun to rise. Kate was in the tiny cubbyhole between the cockpit and the kitchenette going through her yoga routine. He propped his head on the pillows and watched. She showered and dressed. On her way to the kitchenette, she stopped and asked, "Why are you still in bed?"

"I'm staying out of the way."

"So, you're ready to get up and start exercising?"

"I guess I'm ready to get up."

"Mac, I would like to see you get in the habit of exercising two or three times a day. I would like you to start the day off with a morning routine."

He pointed to his head. "Again. Normal rules don't apply."

"I will consider myself successful if you are able to visit with your cousin when we reach his or her house. I will consider myself extremely successful if I can get you comfortably situated after the visit."

Success? That had never occurred to him. He had no idea how to define it. He shrugged. Kate continued,

"Think of this as a marathon. You can improve your odds of finishing it by doing a few simple things. Eating right, exercising, and getting enough rest."

"The doctors said I could extend my life by a year or more with radiation and chemotherapy, but I would be bedridden before I actually died."

She nodded. "Unfortunately, that's true." She fixed him with a laser stare. "There are alternatives. For example, you could combine traditional treatment with homeopathic practices. That's what you would get at St. Elizabeth's."

Mac shook the suggestion off without waiting to hear the rest. "Would that cure my cancer?"

"It could offer you a better chance of staying alive longer, just like traditional oncology. You would find the experience more agreeable. But the goal is survival, not a cure."

"Do you think I should give it a try?"

"That's up to you. It's a decision only you can make."

"If I went that route, the first thing they would do is see if the tumor was growing back. Then they would have to operate again. Then they would insist on chemo and radiation therapy."

"Probably."

"And if I wait until I finish this trip, it will be too late."

Kate pressed her lips into a line and nodded. Mac said, "Once I checked myself into a treatment program like that, I'd be as good as dead. I'll stick with my plan."

"That's why I'm suggesting a second alternative."

"Which is?"

"You commit to the program of diet, exercise, and rest that I have in mind."

"What if I don't?"

"I'm only a couple of hundred miles from home. You agree now, or I start figuring out how to get back to St. Louis."

"Go ahead," he sneered.

She smiled. "You're a stubborn old goat, but you're not a fool. I'm your backup in case something goes wrong."

"You're something else, woman."

"Come on, Mac. I'm not trying to take over your life. I am just trying to get you to take care of yourself, so you can enjoy it."

He threw his hands up. "Shit."

"Are you going to do what I ask?"

Mac closed his eyes and shook his head. "Yeah."

Kate put on her sternest face. "Okay. Let's get started."

He didn't budge. She said, "You just said you would."

Mac rolled into a sitting position. His legs dangled over the edge of the bed. "Come on," Kate urged.

"I've got to pee."

"I'll wait."

When he got back from the bathroom, she said, "You'll have to stow the bed to give yourself some room."

He glared. She watched impassively with her arms folded across her chest. Mac shrugged and stowed the bed. She moved toward the center of the cabin and stood facing him. "This is the Greeting to the Sun."

She bent over, placed her palms flat on the floor and extended her legs back into a front leaning rest. She pushed her hips up and back, then lowered her body parallel to the floor but not resting on it. Her head and shoulders raised up until she was looking at the ceiling. Her torso bent sharply at the waist to form an 'L.' Then she reversed the moves, stood, and raised her hands to the ceiling in a graceful flourish.

"I can't do that," Mac grumped.

"We're about to create MacGregor's Greeting to the Sun. How far down can you stretch?"

He bent over. His hands hung near the middle of his shins. She pushed gently on his back. "See if you can reach your ankles."

He couldn't. But Kate made him hold the stretch while she counted to ten. "Get down on your hands and knees."

His knees creaked painfully as he bent to reach the floor. Pain shot through them as soon as he put his weight on them. "Shit," he bellowed. "Fucking shit."

"What's the matter?"

"This hurts like hell."

"Do you want a pad for your knees? A pair of your jeans would probably work."

"Nah." He grimaced. "Let's get this over with."

She placed one hand on the small of his back and the other on his chest. "Pull your head up and back to look at the ceiling. Hold. One. Two. Three."

She moved her hand to the back of his head. "Roll your head into your chest. Arch your back like a cat and suck your stomach in. Hold. One. Two. Three. Now get into a front leaning rest like you're going to do a pushup."

Mac slid his feet back and as straight and rigid as he could. Pain shot through both shoulders as soon as the weight hit them. His right shoulder hadn't had time to heal from the bullet. The left was complaining about some forgotten strain. "Ahh. Shit," Mac hissed.

"You okay?"

"I'll live."

Kate shook her head and pressed on. She put a hand on his lower back and one on his chest. "Pull your head and shoulders back to look at the ceiling while you let your belly sink toward the floor. Hold. One. Two. Three. Now back to your hands and knees. Pull one foot up."

Mac drew his left knee up to his chest. He had to grab his ankle to pull his foot into position. "Stand."

His thigh balked at the effort, but he managed to raise his body and drag his right foot up for support. He pushed into a standing position. Kate held his right arm to make sure he didn't fall. "And reach for the ceiling. Hold. One. Two. Three. Great. You've got it but let's do it one more time."

10

Kate was making breakfast. Mac was at the table in the cabin. She asked, "How's your memory?."

"Where's this going?"

"It's just a question." She didn't turn to look. The meal held her attention. Their toast was ready to pop and the omelet was almost done. "People your age have problems remembering. Sometimes serious problems."

"Passable. My memory is going just like my vision and hearing, but it's good enough."

"Are there things you can't remember?"

"How would I know?"

"There are events, names, places that you know you should remember. Do you have trouble recalling them?"

"I've always had trouble remembering names. That isn't old age."

"Do you remember people you met in St. Louis?"

"I remember Jimmy."

"Jimmy who?"

"Your cousin, the lawyer. Jimmy Graham."

"Who else?"

"Sam from the diner."

"Last name?" Kate turned to get his response. Mac shrugged and shook his head. "Reinhart," she snapped.

Mac nodded, "Okay."

"Sam from the diner is not a name."

"How do you think we got names like Baker and Smith?"

The mansplaining struck a nerve. Kate whirled and fixed Mac with a withering stare. He ignored her and continued, "Those are occupational names. Somebody way back when was Tom the baker or John the smithy."

The toast popping up brought Kate back to their meal. It was ready. As she dished the eggs onto plates, she asked, "Remember anybody else?"

"The kid running the RV camp. What was it? Discovery Park?"

Kate set their breakfast on the table. Toast, blueberry jelly, a dill pickle, and the omelet split between them. "Camp Discovery. What's his name?"

"Can't come up with it right now. I can describe him. Army vet, Special Forces. Bad arm and a medical discharge from a combat wound. Winning smile. Dark complexion. Muscular like he's done a lot of weight training."

"Eddie?"

"Yeah. Eddie. Same last name as the Raider's coach, but I can't think of his name either."

She studied him while she tried to figure out his thought process. "Flores?" Then she chuckled. "Oh yeah. Tom Flores. I hadn't made that connection."

"That was a long time ago. How would you know that?"

Kate flashed a self-satisfied grin and snickered, "1983. I was one. But Superbowl history was an important subject when I was in high school." She flipped back to serious. "What's the most important event you remember?"

Mac didn't hesitate. "I was drafted in September 67 and sent over to Nam shortly after Christmas."

She nodded. "I meant in terms of world history like the Kennedy assassination."

"I remember both Kennedy assassinations. I also remember the assassination of Martin Luther King. But only as things I've read about. 9/11 is different. I was in Manhattan when those planes crashed into the World Trade Center."

Kate stopped eating and stared, crushed by her own memories.

"I also remember the day US forces pulled out of Saigon," the old man said. "I wasn't there, and I don't remember the date, but I remember terrified Vietnamese fighting desperately to escape the inevitable."

"Do you have any good memories?"

"Shortly after I returned to college, this girl I had dated a couple of times came up and threw her arms around me. I hugged her back, and she said, 'Where have you been?'"

"That's pretty amazing. I'm going out on a limb here. Her name was Anne."

"Anne Campbell. She was still in school because she had been two years behind me when I was drafted."

"Do you remember when you decided to get married?"

"Can't pinpoint the date. I'm sure we were both ready before I asked her."

"Do you remember asking her?"

Mac beamed. He laughed. "I was invited to Cherry Hill for an interview in April, and I got an offer in May. I went over to her house and showed her the letter, then I asked her to marry me." He looked down. Eyes shut. Shit-eating grin. "She said, 'Yes.' We undressed each other and made love for the first time."

"That would be hard to forget."

Mac finished his eggs and daydreamed. His head nodded or shook a memory away every so often. His face tensed in concentration then relaxed. Kate watched. He paused to stare at her while he finished chewing a bite of toast. He took a sip of coffee and said, "I don't remember the date. I think it was in '93 or '94. The Department of Justice sent a team to interview Reagan about some of the shenanigans that took place while he was in office."

"That was 1990. It was a deposition on behalf of Poindexter."

"As I recall, he talked a lot about his movie career but couldn't remember what happened while he was in office."

"I guess. The videotape was used in the Poindexter trial."

"When I saw the tape on TV, I decided the man was suffering from dementia. A couple of years later, he issued a public announcement confirming that he had Alzheimer's."

"Your point?"

"My memory is like that. I don't think I'm that bad. But I'm clearly having problems."

"How do you feel about that?"

"It sucks, but what am I going to do?"

"Work to hang onto your memory as long as you can."

"I've found that it's best to ignore problems you can't fix."

The plan for the day included the Arrow Rock State Historic Site and Fort Osage. Mac decided to visit Clark's Hill, about 20 miles on the other side of Jefferson City before heading north. Clark didn't own the hill. The Corps was camped at its base near the juncture of the Osage and Missouri rivers. He hiked to the top. In his diary, he described the view as "delightful."

Ideas washed over Mac like floodwaters as he stood at the top and surveyed the countryside. He told Kate the spot was a history book waiting to be written down. "I'll bite," she said. "Give me a quick summary."

"Clark's camp was at the bottom of this hill where the two rivers ran together. Two hundred years later, that confluence has moved miles downstream. The face of the earth is constantly changing."

Pointing out a couple of nearby burial mounds, he said, "According to my book, these mounds have been here for more than two thousand years. There's a lot of history behind how they got here and why they are still here."

"Look out there," he said, opening his arms to the woodland panorama. "All that belonged to the aboriginal Americans when Europeans arrived. Those people were primitive, but they had a viable society. We've replaced it with our complex, overly busy post-industrial society." The thought infuriated him. "I've read that hunter-gatherers only had to work about twenty hours a week. Modern American families need two people working forty hours a week to make it."

He turned to Kate. "Are we really making progress?"

She sighed and looked around. "I see weeds, Mac. Acres and acres of weeds. There are snakes out there. Bugs. Ticks. The bugs would eat us alive if we walked around in those weeds."

"Yeah. You're right. No point in wasting time here."

"I didn't mean it that way. We can stay if you want."

"It wouldn't do any good."

"It's just not my thing, Mac."

"You're right. We need to keep moving."

Mac insisted on driving when they got back in the camper. He took them on state roads that wound through the countryside along the river except for a short stretch on I-70. Neither said a word.

The Arrow Rock Historic Site occupied a tidy brick building. Its collection of artifacts from centuries of life in the American Midwest offered an opportunity to linger and learn. But they settled for lunch at the historic tavern across the street.

Kate insisted on driving to Fort Osage, so Mac could rest. He picked up her tablet and looked it over. He had seen them but never held one. It was smaller than his laptop. It didn't have handy stuff like a keyboard and a DVD player. He gave her an accusing look. "You were using this to read on the way to Arrow Rock."

"Yes. It helps me pass the time."

"You bored already?"

"No. I'm enjoying the scenery."

"Pretty hard to read and watch the road."

"I wouldn't attempt to read while driving. But I've always been able to read and do other things at the same time."

"What are you reading?"

"*Stormy Seas*. It's about a woman privateer in the eighteenth century."

"I bet a woman wrote it."

"What's wrong with that? Women have written some of the best books of all time."

"Do you think I'd like it?"

"I don't know. It's pretty good." She looked over at Mac and grinned. "You can read it if you'd like."

A minute or so later, Kate said, "I'll pair the tablet with your audio system tonight, and we can listen to a book together. You pick the book."

"How about *Call of the Wild*?"

"That's a good one. I read it years ago."

"So, you wouldn't want to listen to it now."

"I would love to listen to it. But you might want to find a contemporary novel with a similar story. Why don't you do a little research before deciding?"

"Hmph"

"Either way, I'll set it up tonight."

Fort Osage was a disappointment. The main attraction was a twentieth-century reconstruction of an early nineteenth-century fort. Actors in costumes portrayed military life as it was two hundred years ago. But without the life and death challenges to spice it up. The tale of the Osage nation stuck out in Mac's mind.

The tribe had been farming along the Osage River and hunting in the nearby woodlands for over a thousand years when Lewis and Clark showed up in 1804. Twenty years later, they ceded their Missouri land to the US government to satisfy the demands of European settlers. Twenty years after that, they were pushed off their reservation in Kansas and forced to settle in Oklahoma. When oil became a big deal, the mineral rights made them wealthy. But they were forced to pay a heavy price for the windfall.

Mac and Kate strolled around the museum giving the displays a cursory review. Artifacts of military life didn't interest either of them. They made plans for the following day over dinner in the camper. Kate set up a reservation at an RV park a few miles outside Nebraska City. She took the Interstate and listened to *Stormy Seas*. Mac slept.

11

K ate got the day started with their morning workout routines. She added some Tai Chi drills to Mac's regimen. He was more cooperative this time. As a young athlete, he had formed the habit of starting his day with calisthenics. He could not remember getting away from the practice, but he was ready to pick it up again.

After breakfast, they drove to the Lewis and Clark Interpretive Trail and Visitor Center a couple of miles away. The three-story-high museum was the heart of a 79-acre park overlooking the Missouri River. Mac was reminded of going to church as he and Kate climbed the concrete walkway from the parking lot. The dominant central structure soared upward to the heavens like a cathedral. On either side, transoms spread like wings.

The museum had been designed to show as well as tell the story of the Lewis and Clark expedition. Walking paths wandered through stands of trees and shrubbery. Bison and other animals had been mounted in settings that displayed them living in their natural habitat. Many of the exhibits were interactive. Visitors could board and explore a full-sized replica of the 55-foot keelboat designed by Lewis and used by the Discovery Corps as a barge to transport themselves and their supplies.

A 32-minute Ken Burns documentary on the Journey of Discovery was screened every hour in the museum's theater.

Thomas Jefferson, one of the bright lights of the 18th Century, pursued wide-ranging interests with great energy. Merriweather Lewis was his star pupil. The young soldier was able to document 178 new plants and 122 new animals during his two-year journey across the northwest corner of what is now the United States. His collection revealed a very different world west of the Mississippi.

French Canadian hunters and trappers like Toussaint Charbonneau, the husband of Sacagawea, most likely knew all about those plants and animals but had no reason to share their knowledge. Indians like Sacagawea had lived their entire lives in that part of the world. They knew the geography well enough to guide the explorers on their journey. They were undoubtedly familiar with the flora and fauna. But the specimens Lewis sent back were a revelation to Jefferson.

Mac and Kate roamed the museum working their way up to the third-floor loft. Hundreds of exhibits were set out in a diorama suggesting the wilderness that greeted the Discovery Corps. Mac paused to survey the montage from the middle of the room and said, "I don't know how to put this."

Kate looked up from a display of prairie flowers. "Put what?"

"I'm overwhelmed and disappointed at the same time."

"What did you expect?"

"A revelation. An aha moment."

"Isn't this a textbook, like Clark's hill?"

"Yes." He nodded. "It tells me what life on the Great Plains was like when Lewis and Clark came through." He shook his head. "But all I get from it is a sense of what we've lost."

"So, if you got a chance to talk to Lewis and Clark, you would tell them 'Great job, but it was a complete waste'?"

"Naw. I've had my share of projects that fell into that category. It's best to forget them."

Mac led Kate down the stairs through the Center to the trails at the back of the building. They followed the Birding Trail, which led to a bluff overlooking the Missouri River. Then they picked up the Limestone Trail that meandered through a stand of trees to another river overlook. They continued along the ridge above the river to the Earth Lodge Trail, which took them back to the museum.

The Plains Indian Earth Lodge Exhibit stood a few yards from the main building. It was a man-made cave that reminded Mac of an igloo. Sod and tree limbs had been artfully piled onto a skeleton constructed from tree trunks. The thick layer of turf and branches sloped away from the roof, forming a hill that protected the occupants from wind and water damage. The entrance was an anteroom seven feet high, seven feet wide and seven feet deep.

Inside, the one-room structure was a marvel of engineering. It was large enough to accommodate a dozen or more people. The main floor was below ground level to take advantage of geothermal effects. Storage spaces for perishables had been crafted into the floor. A fireplace sat in the center of the room directly below a smoke-exhaust hole in the roof. Platforms had been set up on a raised level running along the outside wall. They were like Captain's beds with sleeping space on top and storage space below.

Kate stopped to read a signboard on her way out of the exhibit. It gave a short write-up on earth lodges. She looked up at Mac and said, "Women built these homes and owned them."

Mac scanned the sign. "Did you notice the beams holding up the roof?"

She shrugged. He continued, "Men cut the logs and put them in place before any other work was done."

"But the lodges belonged to the *women* because *they* built them."

"I guess that proves women have always been capable builders when they wanted to do the work." He paused and smiled. "But women in Europe and Asia were smart enough to get men to do the work for them."

"A woman can do anything a man can do."

Mac nodded. "But for centuries, they didn't. Chimpanzees are the same. Female chimps can fight as well as males, but they send the men out on patrol to guard their territory."

"Men run the world. Women put up with it to survive."

"Some men do. Most trudge through life, struggling to keep themselves and their families afloat." Mac chuckled. "You know what they say, 'Behind every successful man, there is a woman.' Women push men to give them what they want. Sometimes that backfires."

"Women were only allowed to work outside the home because men were off fighting wars. Wars which, by the way, men started. We had to fight for the right to vote."

"Men had to fight for the right to vote as well. You just don't remember that part of it. Democracy began in Sparta when men refused to serve in the army unless they had a say in running the state."

"Why just men?" Kate howled. "Shouldn't the women have a say as well?"

"You would have to ask them. I wasn't around at the time."

"Mac, Abigail Adams lobbied for women's rights back in 1776 when the Constitution was drawn up. The framers ended up with *all men*, but they meant all *white* men."

"You're right. We *white* men have fucked things up."

"What's that supposed to mean?"

"It means I concede your point. *White* men like me are a plague."

"That's condescending."

"There's only one way this ends: you're right, and I'm wrong."

"Stop patronizing me. You *are* wrong."

"I accept that. If you want me to kiss the ground in obeisance, forget it. I wouldn't be able to get up after I got down there."

She sneered, "You can be a real ass."

Another spell hit. He was suddenly light-headed, woozy. He closed his eyes and felt himself totter. Weakness spread upward from his legs through his chest and shoulders. The sun burned his skin like a heat lamp. These sensations passed in seconds. "Yeah. Look, I'm going back to the camper."

"What is wrong with you?"

"I'm a white man. That's not going to change. If you don't like it, go home. I'll pay for the flight."

"Don't be ridiculous. You're in no condition to drive to your cousin's home in Alaska. You need me."

"I don't need this. Get me a fucking gun. I'll put an end to it right now, and you can stop worrying about me."

"Mac!"

He was ready to call it quits. Blowing his brains out would have been no problem if he had a gun. He had decided against that months ago. Now he was wondering if he had made the right decision. He started back to the camper.

Kate caught up before he reached the museum steps. She planted herself in front of him. "What's going on, Mac? I was just talking to you."

Mac looked up at the building looming in front of him. He still had to make it through the museum and out to the parking lot. That might be more than he could manage. He took deep breaths fighting for control. "I'm tired of talking."

"Can't I talk to you about what it's like to be a woman in this society?"

"You can talk about anything you want. But I can't stand people who have to win conversations."

He moved to go around her, but she moved with him. "What does that mean?"

"It means that you had to vent and decided to make me your scapegoat."

"I did nothing of the kind."

"I tried to end the conversation. You wouldn't let it go. Now I'm trying to get back to the RV, and you're blocking me."

Kate took a step to the side. "I'm sorry."

Mac walked past her. She called out, "Where are you going?"

"To get a drink."

"What about me?"

"That's your problem." He shrugged. "Book a flight to St. Louis."

Mac was feeling normal by the time he had worked his way through the displays on the first floor. He paused and looked around when he reached the door. Kate was a few steps behind. He held the door until she caught up before he walked out onto the front stoop.

He went straight to the back of the camper for his usual half cup of scotch. Kate went to the front. She puttered around while he made himself comfortable on the sofa. After a few minutes, she came to the back. "I've got your book set up."

"My book?"

"Your audiobook, *Call of the Wild.*"

He looked up at her. "And?"

"I thought we could listen to it while I drive up to Council Bluffs."

He took a drink and savored the fire as it went down. *Never admit you're wrong. Never apologize.* He pulled the keys out of his pocket and handed them to her.

12

all of the Wild is an exciting story but it wasn't
the right selection for Mac's mood on the ride
up to Council Bluffs. The story of good old Buck
being kidnapped and shipped off to Alaska for life
as a sled dog deepened his funk. It brought back the
draft, training and shipping off to Vietnam.

His first memory was a bus ride on a hot, muggy
night. Lights were on in the cottages along the road.
The locals were working deep into the night. When
he and the others deboarded, they were directed to a
nearby tent and told to find a bunk. He had to feel his
way around in the tent's pitch-black interior. Outside
artillery fire punctuated by explosions boomed nonstop.

After breakfast the next morning, he was assigned
to a sand bag detail. He spent his first day in-country
filling sand bags and building a defensive wall under a
blistering equatorial sun. The work didn't bother him.
He was used to working outside in summer heat. But
it was Sunday, and he was not allowed to go to church.
That irked him. It still bothered him. He couldn't say
why. He no longer attended Mass.

The Lewis and Clark Monument at Council Bluff honors the first meeting between the Captains and Native American leaders. The historic meeting took place in the summer of 1804, about three months into the journey. President Jefferson had ordered the captains to set up friendly contacts with the Indigenous People. When the expedition reached the mouth of the Platte River, Lewis decided to take a break and look for some Indians.

The first attempt was a flop. Scouts from the Discovery Corps located a village but it was empty. The inhabitants were out hunting buffalo.

Lewis proceeded a few miles north to what is now Omaha, Nebraska. This time his men successfully connected with the Otoe. The following day, Lewis, Clark and their interpreters met with minor chiefs. The real leaders didn't have time for them. Lewis gave a long speech. The part about the prosperity the new rulers of the land would bring appealed to the Native American audience. But they had already heard the same promises from the British, the French, and the Spanish.

The Western Historic Trails Center was a flat, round building on the east bank of the Missouri River just south of I-80 in Council Bluffs. A concrete walk led from the parking lot to an interlaced stone pathway. A sign at the edge of the reddish stone walk welcomed visitors "to the story of America's trails west."

They passed a very large black granite sculpture as they approached the museum building. It had the jagged edge of a piece of paper that had been ripped from a larger sheet. Peaks and valleys along the top depicted the topology of the 1800-mile journey from the Mississippi to the Pacific. Its right edge rose rapidly from the river valley to the undulating Great Plains. Left of center, it peaked in Montana as the trail crossed the Rockies before plunging precipitously to the ocean at the left edge.

Kate and Mac wandered around the museum taking in the exhibits before going outside to a patio that provided a view of the river and the woodlands on both banks. As they walked, Mac ranted, "This is all well and good but it skips over the fundamental problem – they didn't know what they were doing." He turned to Kate and shook his head. She couldn't tell if he was mad or just frustrated. He fumed, "Yes, they did a good job as they understood the mission. Jefferson wanted to get along with the indigenous peoples but he wasn't prepared to deal with them. Neither Meriwether Lewis nor William Clark was a qualified diplomat." He paused to collect his thoughts. "Jefferson's biggest problem was that he did not understand the Europeans flooding into his country. He hadn't realized that the European worldview was incompatible with the Native American worldview."

Kate smirked. "East is East, and West is West, and never the twain shall meet."

After a long silence, Kate said, "I have a question." Mac turned to her. Her eyes stayed focused on a spot across the river. "What did you and Anne fight about?"

"We didn't."

"All married couples fight."

"We didn't. Anne was too smart. She got what she wanted without fighting."

Kate turned, eyes wide in disbelief. "She wore the pants in your house? Com'on, Mac."

"It wasn't like that. We got along fine. We took care of each other. But she knew how to deal with people. Especially me."

"Still sounds like she had you under her thumb."

"I see your point but that doesn't sound like us." Mac leaned back and closed his eyes. He struggled to come up with the right way to explain the situation. "I've read that the problem in marriage is getting two adults with different goals and different agendas to work together." He waited for a response but Kate just watched him with her laser stare. "There are three ways it can work. He dominates and she goes along. She dominates and he goes along. Or they figure out how to negotiate and compromise." Mac took a deep breath and let the air out slowly. "My recollection is that we compromised. And I'm pretty sure that was because of Anne."

Kate mumbled, "I suppose."

"You don't believe me?"

"I'm jealous. You were married forty years and you're still in love with her." Her lip curled into a sneer. "I can't even get a relationship to last a year."

"Do you want to talk about it?"

She shook her head. "Tell me something about Anne."

He studied the clouds floating lazily overhead as he leafed through memories. "Ever read *Cheaper by the Dozen*?"

"Hasn't everybody?"

He chuckled, "I doubt that most people have." He flashed a grin. "Anyway, it was Anne's bible. Lillian Gilbreth was her hero."

"You only had two children."

"Anne decided two was a good number. She had her tubes tied after our Ann was born."

"Her decision or a negotiation?"

"She told me what she was going to do. As I recall the discussion came down to: I didn't have to carry them and I didn't have to raise them but I would have to pay for college."

"So you went along."

"I would have gone along anyway. I could see all of that without her telling me. My only question was whether she was sure that's what she wanted."

"As opposed to you getting a vasectomy?"

"Never came up. I suppose I would have agreed to it but it wouldn't have changed anything."

"It would have been your body instead of hers."

"Over the years she sometimes regretted her decision. Just a passing whim. She would have had the same regrets if I was the one who couldn't deliver."

"You didn't have any regrets?"

"Naw. Kids are a lot of work and a lot of trouble. I'm glad we had two but I didn't need any more. It's different for women. They see a little baby and imagine how nice it would be to have one of their own."

Kate grimaced and shook her head. Mac brought the conversation back to her. "What's wrong with Eddie?"

"Nothing. Why?'

"You said you had dated him. Why'd you stop?"

She glared. "You sound like my parents. 'Why aren't your married? You're gonna end up a lonely old spinster.'"

"I'm sorry. I was just wondering about two people I kinda like."

She calmed down a notch but the anger in her voice was unmistakable. "He's busy. I'm busy. We don't need a relationship."

Mac nodded. "That's true. I will say, however, as someone who has been married most of his life: the plusses outweigh the minuses."

"You were lucky."

"And you're not?"

"I've had some bad luck."

"For instance?"

Kate tensed and turned to look off into the distance. She shook her head. "The last guy put me in the hospital."

"How bad?"

"They carried me in on a stretcher. I had a concussion, two broken ribs and a punctured lung. I had to drop out of nursing school while I recovered."

"I guess that would sour me on dating."

She sneered, "Yeah."

"Why didn't you go back to school? That's what I would have done."

"How would you know?"

"I was a senior in college when I got the draft notice. I spent a year in Vietnam. All I wanted to do when I got out was finish my degree."

"I planned to finish. I was working at the VA hospital in D.C. when it happened. My family got me to move to St. Louis with Jimmy to get away from the guy. I started working at St. Elizabeth's and never got around to going back."

They sat staring at the trees and the river. Mac kept thinking about this beautiful young woman wasting her life, while a couple of miles away, a great young guy was whiling away his time on busy work. He wanted them to get together and make a life for themselves. He wondered out loud, "So why would you just drop everything and take off on a wild goose chase with a total stranger?"

"Why not? I needed a change. You needed help."

"For a hundred dollars a day? You could be making a lot more than that."

She laughed. "I'm not doing this for the money, Mac."

"Why are you doing it?"

"I like you. I've liked you from the moment I laid eyes on you. I might even be in love with you."

He shook his head. "A little late for that. I had a good run with Anne. I'm not looking for a new Mrs. MacGregor."

"Got it. I'm not looking for anything. I'm just telling you how I feel."

Mac grunted. "You should be looking for a young guy who can make you happy."

"I've found a guy who makes me happy. He's an irascible old Scot."

"Who's pretty near the end."

"But you aren't waiting for it to come and cart you away. You're fighting for every last minute." She smiled at him. "Those others, the one's at St. Elizabeth's, only have a short time but they don't know what to do with it." She took his hand and kissed it. "We have had more adventure in the last couple of days than some people have in their entire lives."

Mac kissed her hand back. "You know. I might be in love with you."

She laughed. "Do you think it might be time to get back on the road?"

"Probably."

Kate bounced to her feet. Mac needed her help to get off the bench. He put an arm around her waist as they walked back to the camper. "You know what would have happened if we had met twenty years ago?"

She shook her head. "No. What?"

"Nothing. I was married to Anne."

"And I was chasing jocks. I didn't have time for old married guys."

13

—

Their next stop was Spirit Mound National Prairie, a couple of hours north of Council Bluffs. Kate set up a reservation at an RV park on the outskirts of Vermillion, South Dakota, a few minutes from Spirit Mound. She started up I-29 with *Call of the Wild* playing in the background.

They paused to visit the monument to Sergeant Floyd when they reached Sioux City, Iowa. He was the only member of the Discovery Corps to die during the two-year wilderness trek. His death resonated with Mac because the sergeant's companions knew he was sick but had no way of helping him. Doctors now believe he had an infected appendix. Back then, medical science was too primitive to make the diagnosis and treat the disease.

His courage in the face of death has captivated Americans through the centuries. His body has been re-buried twice since his death. Now a towering monument stands watch over his latest gravesite. That's an amazing amount of work just to preserve the memory of a minor historical figure killed by an appendage with no known value.

Kate studied the sandstone obelisk. "How tall is that thing?"

"A hundred feet."

"It's an odd monument for a military man."

Mac said, "It might have been the inspiration for the Vietnam Memorial."

"I've visited the Wall. It's magnificent. There's no comparison."

"We had a lot more money to spend when we put up the Vietnam War Memorial. It's a bauble to distract us from what really happened."

"We were defending our way of life."

Mac smirked. "We were afraid the Russians and the Chinese would take over Southeast Asia." His face curled in disgust. "Vietnam was a little guy caught in the middle."

"What does that say about our soldiers who fought the war?"

"Used and abused," he sneered. "For the most part, we were good men who fought courageously and conducted ourselves honorably. But we were fighting a bad war."

"So does the Wall honor our heroes or not?"

"Heroes and non-heroes alike. One sergeant from my company took his M-14 into the latrine, stuck the barrel in his mouth, and pulled the trigger." Mac sucked in a breath and huffed it out. "Officers and men were fragged by guys who had it in for them. One man was killed in an industrial accident. He was electrocuted when the steel beam he was unloading from a flatbed bumped against a power line. Hell, I almost died in a traffic accident."

"You?"

"I had to drive staff officers up to Kon Tum a couple of times a month. Some general issued orders for our convoy to move at 25 miles per hour. So we were cruising along a mountain road when all hell broke loose. Machine guns were firing from the hill on our left. Mid-air explosions like Fourth of July fireworks lit up the sky on our right. The Armored Personnel Carrier in front took off. A soldier leaned out the left side and pumped his arm. Double Time. I hit the gas. I looked back. The deuce-and-a-half behind me was coming fast. When I turned back to the road, I saw this Vietnamese Lambretta pulling from the left shoulder into the gap between me and the APC. If I hit that sucker, the truck would crush me, the jeep, and my boss. I tamped the brakes. That bought me enough time to skid around behind it. Then I floored the accelerator."

"Sounds pretty heroic."

"As opposed to avoiding assholes on Maryland highways?"

Kate grimaced. "Why do you have such a shitty attitude?"

"The invasion and occupation of South Vietnam was an atrocity, and I was forced to help make it happen."

Kate studied him but said nothing. Mac continued, "Anybody with any sense should have realized it was a no-win situation."

"We beat the Germans. Why not the Vietnamese?"

"We were *stalemated* in Korea," Mac growled. "If we had defeated the North Vietnamese, we would have needed a military presence to keep a lid on things. The Vietnamese would have done everything they could to kick us out like they did the French. American moms would have demanded that we bring our boys home. That's not a win."

"Kennedy had been building up troop support for Diem and the South Vietnamese almost from the moment he took office."

"It wasn't working. Kennedy could see that. So could Johnson." Mac paused to scan the monument. His mouth was clamped shut. His hands clenched in tight fists. He turned back to Kate. "LBJ should have pulled our troops out as soon as he won the election in 64."

"South Vietnam would have collapsed."

Mac wanted to say the South collapsed anyway. But nothing came out. He was overwhelmed by the horror of it all. In 68, Johnson dropped out. Robert Kennedy was assassinated. Nixon took over the country. Tens of thousands of American men were killed or survived with missing limbs and debilitating mental scars. Vietnam Stress Syndrome became a thing. Mac knew all about that. He had lived with it. Probably still did. He was shaking uncontrollably. Tears welled up. He turned to get back to the camper.

Kate caught him and folded him into her arms. She pulled his cheek to hers and held tight, soothing him with the seductive touch of her soft, warm skin and the delicious scent of her Eau de Cologne. When he had come back from the edge, she took his hand. They walked to the camper. She settled him on the sofa and fetched his scotch. He sipped. She kissed him on the cheek. "I'm going to drive us to the camp-site. Okay?"

He nodded. "Yeah."

By the time they reached the RV park, the sun was setting. It was dinnertime. As soon as they were situated, they got out for a walk. Kate asked, "What did you think of *Call of the Wild?*"

"Not much of a story, but London certainly made it exciting. Lots of action."

"I liked it."

Mac nodded. "I didn't dislike it, but I didn't need all the violence. The ending was nice with Old Buck leading the wolf pack and having his way with the she-wolves."

"You're jealous of Buck."

"You're damn right. Why not?"

"He's stuck in a harsh, dangerous life. He has to hunt for his food and fight his rivals. What's the attraction?"

"That's what wolves do. They've lived that way for forty million years. Buck gets to hunt and fight and, pardon my French, fuck?"

"Would you really like to live that way?"

"I couldn't now. I believe I might have in my prime. That's how my ancestors lived."

Kate smiled skeptically. "A long time ago."

"Probably not as long ago as you imagine. Native Americans were living like that when the Pilgrims got here."

"But you've never actually done it."

"I was trained in the Infantry. We spent a lot of time on field exercises. I liked that part of it."

"What happened?"

"When I got to Nam, the CO needed a driver. I got the job. My responsibilities were to chauffeur him around and take care of the equipment."

"That doesn't sound bad."

"It wasn't, given that I had to spend a year over there fighting a war I knew was stupid and immoral."

"Otherwise, you might have made it a career?"

"I could very well have made a career of the Army if the circumstances had been right."

"Because of the killing or the sex?"

"The sex is a plus." He rubbed his chin. "The killing doesn't appeal to me. It's the danger and the challenges."

They stopped at a picnic table a few yards from their camper. Kate said, "Hold that thought. I'm going to get us some dinner."

Mac sat watching the sun go down like the dying flame on a candle. Night creatures emerged as daylight faded to darkness. Crickets chirped. Bugs took to the air. A few bats flitted around, feasting on them. Lightening bugs blinked on and off as they went about their business. The stars were beginning to shine. Soon, the Big Dipper, the Little Dipper, and the North Star would be visible.

Kate returned with hot dogs, beans, and beer. The food went fast. They lingered over the beer. Stars filled the night sky. The symphony of night creature sounds played in the background. Kate interrupted the reverie. "When did you and Anne stop having sex?"

"Ten or twelve years ago."

"You were still pretty young. What happened?"

"I got a back injury – a ruptured disk. I had to sleep sitting up for several weeks. When I started sleeping with her again, sex was a chore."

"You or her?"

"She was tense and fought me. I think she was afraid it was going to hurt. When I did get in, I worked hard, but nothing happened. It was too much for both of us, so I gave up."

She fixed him with her laser stare. "Are you capable of consummating sex?"

Mac nodded. "Yes."

"When was the last time?"

"A month or so ago."

"You met someone after Anne's death?"

"Two someones."

"What happened?"

"Marie Johnson pushed me to start chemo. We had sex a couple of times before the treatments began. She broke up with me when I told her I wasn't going to continue them."

"And that's when you decided on this trip."

He shook his head. "I began planning the trip before I quit the treatments. I wanted her to come along with me."

They went back to watching the stars. Darkness deepened around them. The moon rose full and bright. When Mac spotted the Big Dipper, he tapped Kate on the shoulder and pointed. She nodded. "I see it."

He said, "I suppose we should go inside."

"Yeah," she agreed. "Time to put you to bed."

They carried their stuff into the camper and Kate started rinsing dishes in the sink. The kitchenette created a bottleneck barely wide enough for two people. When Mac tried to pass her on his way to the cabin, Kate stretched, pushing her rear end back. Mac was trapped. He turned sideways to slide past her. She pressed her butt into his crotch. He looked around, trying to figure out the best way to handle the situation. Suddenly, Kate whirled, threw her arms around him and kissed him on the lips. He grabbed her butt and pulled her close. Her clit worked up and down against his jeans. His cock stiffened.

Her mouth opened inviting penetration. His tongue slid over hers. Kisses on her neck, shoulder, and chest were rewarded with soft moans. She reached down and stroked the bulge in his pants. Mac turned her around. As she leaned over Kate's hands came to rest on the edge of the sink.

Mac got his pants out of the way. Then hers. The whole time he kept wondering, *Has it always been this hard?* He was ready to give it up, but she looked back. Her eyes urged him to keep going. She moaned. Her breath came in short gasps. She was soft and wet. Even so, pushing up inside her was daunting. Old feelings returned once he did make it in, but getting from almost there to a small climax took forever.

When it was over, Mac pulled back. Kate turned around and hugged him. They danced over to the sofa in a clumsy two-step and fell in a heap. He muttered, "I'm sorry that was such an ordeal."

She stroked his cheek. "I've got no complaints."

Mac passed out quickly. Around three, he woke to find Kate sleeping next to him with an arm and a leg draped across his body. He tried to work free without disturbing her. She woke up, smiled, and crawled over him to gain the floor. He got to his feet and shuffled off to the bathroom. By the time he came out, she had set up the bed. Her sleeping bag was rolled up in a corner.

14

Kate woke at six - a habit she had developed because her shift at St. Elizabeth's started at seven. Her normal routine was exercise, breakfast, shower, dress, and off to work. Sleeping arrangements in the camper had required her to crawl over Mac without waking him before going into her exercise routine.

This morning she paused to pay attention to the man sharing her bed. She listened to his snoring. Watched his chest rise and fall. Marveled at the peaceful, carefree expression on his face. She leaned in and gave him a light peck on the cheek. "Good morning."

The snoring stopped. Mac's eyes opened. After a moment, he turned and looked at Kate. "Good morning."

She crawled over him to get up and get started. As she did, he wrapped an arm around her head and pulled her in for a proper kiss. She obliged then pushed off. She let him lie and watch her work through her yoga routine. "Okay, Mac. Time to get moving."

Mac rolled grudgingly out of bed, lumbered to the bathroom and returned for his morning misery.

They discussed plans for the day over breakfast. The Spirit Mound National Prairie was a ten-minute drive north on SD-19. The path to the mound began at the edge of a parking lot a short distance from the highway. According to one website, visitors typically spent forty-five minutes checking out the view.

Mac said, "It's a mile-and-a-half from the parking lot to the top of the hill and back. That'll take forty-five minutes."

"Do you want to skip it?"

"Nah. We've come this far."

"It's a four-to-five-hour drive to the Teton Council Site. We should pick another book before we take off."

"Okay."

"What are you interested in? I've got a lot of chick books."

"How about a Western – a cowboy story."

Kate did a search and turned the tablet so Mac could see the result. He pointed to *Hondo* by Louis L'Amour. "This'll be good. I saw the movie when it came out."

It was mid-morning when they parked the RV near the footpath. The weather was typical for May – sunny and mild. Mac got out and stood staring at the small hill in the distance. Kate asked, "You okay?"

"Yeah. It just looks like a long walk."

"We don't have to do it."

"I can't let fear run my life."

With that Mac stepped onto the dirt trail and started his march to the summit. After a while, he said, "This is better than August. Lewis and his buddies walked three hours in the hot sun. Nearly killed'em."

"They were young. They could get away with that. You can't."

At the top, Mac had to recuperate. He sat on a wooden hexagon that marked the summit. Kate handed him an energy bar and a bottle of water. "Eat that and drink the water."

When he had finished, Mac stood to look around. Kate took his hand. "Wow. I never imagined that much empty space."

A sea of prairie grass rippled in the wind. Mountains rose up on the far shore. "Just like it was when Lewis and Clark stood here two hundred years ago," Kate said.

"Except for the large herds of buffalo and elk." Mac pointed to his left where SD-19 was visible. "And a highway connecting us to civilization."

The wilderness treasure was not properly appreciated in America's early years. The prairie had been exploited for commercial gain. The Spirit Mound Historic Prairie was created in 1986 as a nod to the area's natural beauty. Over the following decades, citizens worked to restore the primitive state of the land.

Mac was reminded of the story of Black Beauty. Except in this version, the pendulum was swinging back. Rapacious, manipulative men were battling to gain access to the resources locked in the protected spaces of America's National Forests, Parks and

Wilderness areas. Their foothold in the White House had enabled them to enjoy astounding, if not terrifying, successes. Spirit Mound National Prairie would probably survive as long as no oil or mineral resources were discovered lying beneath the surface.

Kate returned to the camper tingling with excitement. She had heard the call of the wild and could not wait to continue the adventure. Mac was stoic. Depressed by his realization of what America had become.

They drove to Yankton, a half-hour west of Vermillion. The city was named for the Dakota Sioux tribe living in the area when Lewis and Clark passed through. Their Chief signed a treaty ceding tribal lands to the US government in 1858 rather than fight a no-win war. In 1861, President Buchanan issued an executive order creating the Dakota Territory and making Yankton its capital. The city has survived as a river port and an important source of natural resources.

Yankton's main attractions - boating, camping, fishing and hiking – didn't interest the pair. They pulled into a Quiki-Mart for gas. Kate bought sandwiches, coffee, and some groceries. When she stepped into the cockpit with the sandwiches and coffee, she said, "I think I should drive."

"I'm okay. I'm good for a couple of more hours."

"You've had a stressful morning."

"You afraid those wee demons shot me with their arrows?"

"Be serious. That hike was exhausting, and you were upset when we left."

Mac nodded. "I get upset, and I probably overreact. But I'm fine now. I'm getting into the story."

"I think you should let me drive."

"We're going to stop at the museum in Chamberlain, right?"

Kate nodded. Mac said, "You can take over then."

She put the coffee in the cupholders and buckled into the passenger seat. But she scowled in protest. "Follow the river. Stay off the Interstate."

"SD-50 all the way."

The highway did not follow the Missouri. It took them west and then north through rolling farmland. There was an occasional town. No cities. The Yankton Reservation was the most significant thing they encountered. Reservation lands made up over half of Charles Mix County, but there was nothing to make them stand out for a stranger passing through.

A couple of hours after leaving Yankton, Mac turned onto I-90 for the last twenty miles into Chamberlain. The mid-afternoon sun was high in the sky. He blinked several times and jerked his head back and forth as though trying to shake something off. He was losing it. The story of Hondo Lane, Angie Lowe, Chief Vittorio and his Apaches droned on. Kate said, "Mac, are you okay?" She could hear the anxiety in her voice.

Mac turned and nodded. "I'm f-f-fine," he slurred.

Kate ordered, "Mac! Pull over!" She unbuckled her seat belt.

He turned to her again. His hands slipped from the steering wheel. His body slumped forward. The RV began weaving erratically. Kate sprang from her seat and grabbed the steering wheel. Horns blared. She pushed Mac upright and vaulted onto his lap.

Kate kicked Mac's foot off the gas pedal and brought the beast under control. It steadied. The honking subsided. No collisions. She still had to get it to the shoulder without hitting anything. When they came to rest, she closed her eyes and breathed – slow deep breaths. But she couldn't stop just yet. A voice in her head was screaming, *"Get him to a hospital. Every second counts."*

Kate climbed into the aisle and unbuckled Mac's seat belt. She crouched and pulled his arms over her shoulders. Raising up, she lifted him from the captain's chair. A few steps toward the sofa were enough to convince her she couldn't carry him that far. She lowered him to the floor as gently as she could. But his eyes popped open as soon as she had him stretched out. He pushed into a sitting position. "Wha' happen'?" His voice was thick. His speech slurred.

"You had a seizure." Kate helped him struggle to his feet. "I want you to go lie down so I can get you to a doctor."

"I'm fffiiine."

Kate pushed him toward the back. "You're not fine."

He didn't move. "I don' nee' ta lie down."

"At least sit in the passenger's seat so I can get us back on the road."

"Where we goin'?"

"Chamberlain. If I can find a hospital. Or Pierre."

He blinked and gave his head a quick shake. "I'm driv'n' to Sham'erlin."

Kate grabbed his shirt and pulled with all her strength. Mac lost his balance and fell toward her. She shoved him into the passenger seat. "You can't drive, Mac. I have to get you to a hospital. Just sit there. It shouldn't take long."

Someone banged on the side of the RV. Kate yelled, "Just a second." She fastened Mac's seat belt and went to the door. A trooper stood waiting for her – big guy, broad shoulders and narrow hips, crew cut red hair, pinkish skin, Aviator sunglasses. "Is everything okay?" he rumbled.

"I have to get my friend to a hospital. He's had a seizure."

After some back and forth, the man came into the cabin and stood over Mac. "Are you okay, sir?"

"Yeah. I'm ffffiiine." But the words didn't sound right.

The trooper turned to Kate. "Follow me."

Moments later, he turned on his flashing lights. His siren began to wail, and he led them onto the highway. They roared off at high speed.

Kate brought the RV to a stop at the emergency entrance of the Sanford Chamberlain Medical Center. Medics charged into the camper. They lifted Mac out onto a gurney and rushed him to the ER.

15

Four doctors and two hours later, the decision was to keep Mac overnight for observation. Dr. Robert Yang had taken over the old man's case as the attending physician. He wanted to operate. "You are going to die very soon unless something is done about that tumor."

Mac was not feeling himself but he wasn't going under the knife without a fight. "I wan' Nurse Gra'am in here for dis discussion."

"She's not a nurse," Yang corrected. He tried to be patient and caring. He couldn't help sounding arrogant and condescending. "She used to be a nursing assistant."

"She's leg'ly responsible fer ma care," Mac retorted. He could tell he was slurring.

"She can't help you in this situation," Yang explained.

The old man mustered all the fury he could manage. "If I don' leave here 'live, she'll contac' ma 'ttorney." Mac paused to catch his breath. "He'll sue."

The doctor stepped out of the room and returned with Kate in tow. She took a seat next to Mac's bed. Yang folded his arms across his chest. "Will you please explain to your client that he needs immediate surgery to remove the tumor from his brain?"

Kate studied him. She turned to her 'client' and considered her response. She turned back to the doctor. "I'm sure you've already explained the situation to him."

"He wants to hear it from you."

"Mac, do you need to hear it from me?"

He worked his mouth like he was dealing with a shot of Novocain. "Nah."

"Then why is she here?" Yang demanded.

"Ma wi'ness. I'm refus'n' surjry."

"Every minute you delay this surgery," the doctor said in a low, threatening voice, "hurts your chances of survival."

Mac forced a harsh laugh. "Surviv'l."

"I believe you have several months or even a year if we can remove that tumor."

"If da surjry don' kill me."

"That is highly unlikely."

"Unlikely?" That didn't come out right. Mac's brain was working. His body wasn't cooperating.

"Without the surgery, you will die in a matter of days."

"Wi' da surjry, migh' nah live dat long."

Yang threw up his hands. "Surgery is always risky."

"Forgedit. I wanna go now."

"You're in no condition to leave. You need care."

"Daz Nurse Gra'am's job."

Yang looked at Kate and shook his head. "I'm keeping him overnight for observation. I'll make a decision about discharging him when I make my morning rounds."

With that, he stalked out. Kate raced after him. When she returned, she sat on the bed next to Mac and kissed him. "Get some rest. I'll get you out of here in the morning."

16

D r. Yang stepped into Mac's room shortly after 10. Interns followed him like ducklings. He paused to study a tablet that displayed results from an early morning checkup. "You seem to be doing quite well for a man in your condition, Mr. McGregor." Whatever emotions he was feeling were hidden behind a mask of serenity. "I changed your medication and signed for your discharge. You can leave as soon as Ms. Graham has gotten your prescription filled." He bowed slightly. "Good luck."

Kate took Mac to the Lakota Indian Museum for lunch and some light exercise. His right side was weak. A hospital issue cane helped him walk. But he still limped.

Mac's vision was more bothersome. He noticed things off to the side disappearing on the drive from the hospital, but he was in a moving vehicle. As he walked around the museum, he became convinced that he could only see straight ahead. He had to turn his head to see what was on his left or his right. He complained to Kate, "I'm goin' blin'. Can' see outta da corner uh ma eyes."

"That's normal. You'll get better."

They browsed the displays and artwork. The gift shop had native arts and crafts on sale. None of it appealed to Mac. Kate took her time checking out the merchandise but didn't buy anything. They were eating lunch when she said, "Mac, you have to make some decisions."

"Such as?"

"Do you want to keep going?"

He scowled. There was a fire in his eyes but his mouth barely moved. "Yeah."

"Do you want to continue on the Lewis and Clark Trail?"

"Yeah."

"Where does your cousin live?"

Mac studied the ceiling for a long time before answering, "Fairbanks. 's on ma computer."

Kate sighed. "That's worse than I imagined." She grimaced. "I figure we'll need five days to reach Fort Clatsop." She shook her head. "And we'll be no closer to your cousin." She put a finger to her lips and turned her head. She studied Mac out of the corner of one eye. "Going straight to Fairbanks would save us a couple of days."

"I wanna finish," Mac insisted. "Wuz da problem?"

"Dr. Yang is worried about you."

"He wanns ta operate," Mac huffed. "Thaz what 'e does."

"He's been in touch with Dr. Jacobs back in Annapolis. The two of them teleconferenced this morning. I sat in." She paused to breathe in and let the air out of her nose. "The tumor is growing back. The medicine you've been taking wasn't working."

"I'm alive."

"Dr. Yang suggested another medicine he likes. Jacobs agreed."

"Bu' yer nah satisfie'."

"These drugs are experimental. They have been shown to work in some cases. But they have also failed in many cases. There is no way to predict what this drug will do in your case."

"I know wha' i' won' do."

Kate recoiled. She closed her eyes and said, "It's a question of time, Mac. Two or three days may be the difference between a good visit with your cousin and a wasted effort."

Mac's face sank into his hands. A great black emptiness seized him. *The trip was a waste. It didn't matter if he made it to Fairbanks. It didn't even matter if he lived another week or another year. No one cared.* He corrected himself. *Kate cared. She got him out of the hospital. She was ready to go on.* He pushed back. It was not in his nature to quit. He looked up. "Dis trip won' be wasted."

Kate watched him. Poker-faced. Unblinking. He tried to smile. "Yer shar'n' i' wi' me. Dat makes i' wor'while." He took her hand and pulled it to his lips. "Da troot. We gah no guarantees. I may nah make i' ta Fairbanks. Maybe neider of us will."

He stood and pulled Kate into his arms. "We stick to da plan."

She put a hand on his head and kissed him long and hard. "You got it."

They made their way back to the camper. Mac limping along with the aid of his cane. Kate walking at his side. Getting into the camper was the challenge. Mac could reach the next step with his left leg. Kate had to help him with the right leg. When they made it to the cockpit, he needed help getting into the passenger seat. She had to buckle his seatbelt.

Kate took her seat and started the engine but sat staring into space. Mac called her back to the moment. "Kate?"

She looked over and gave him a quick teary-eyed smile. She wiped her eyes with the back of her hand. "Let's go check out that meeting with the Sioux."

She turned on *Hondo* and started north on SD-50 paralleling the east bank of the Missouri. At Fort Thompson, she crossed the river and picked up SD-1806. That took them directly to Fort Pierre, the approximate location of the meeting between Lewis and Clark and Chief Black Buffalo.

Fort Pierre was both a suburb and a historic site. As an urban area, sitting across the river from Pierre, the Stanley County seat, it had about 2000 residents. As a historic site, it boasted several tourist attractions, including Fischers Lily Park, where the meeting with the Lakota took place. Kate was able to get them an RV pad at the park for their overnight stay.

Hondo was in a pickle when they stopped for the night. He had killed Angie's husband Ed in a shootout, then he was captured by the Apaches, who condemned him to a slow, painful death. He was spared when one of the Indians discovered a picture of Angie's son Johnny in his saddlebag. But Angie had to claim Hondo was her man to satisfy Chief Vittorio. That left Hondo with the nasty task of telling Angie and Johnny what happened to Ed.

17

In the morning, they drove to Bismarck for a stop at Fort Abraham Lincoln. The garrison was initially built in 1872 to provide military support for the expansion of the Northern Pacific Railway into Montana. It was abandoned and dismantled in 1895. Teddy Roosevelt signed the land over to North Dakota to become the Fort Abraham Lincoln State Park in 1907. Reconstruction was begun by the Civilian Conservation Corps in 1934.

The original fort was expanded to house the 7th Cavalry in 1873 when Lt Col George Custer was appointed post commander - a position he held until his death at the Battle of the Little Bighorn in 1876.

The main exhibit at the fort was a replica of the army barracks used by Custer and his men. Mac wasn't interested. He had spent too much time living in actual army barracks.

Kate insisted on touring the replica of Custer's house. She wanted to know what life was like for Libbie, the Colonel's wife.

They walked from Custer's house to a replica Mandan village about a half-mile away. The exhibit had five earth lodges and interpretive signs to give some insight into the Mandan way of life. It is believed their settlement at this location near the juncture of the Heart and Missouri rivers had thrived for over two hundred years. At its peak, it may have been home to a thousand people living in 70 or more earth lodges. Now it was a ghost village. The energy generated by an active community of industrious people was missing.

Even when Lewis and Clark arrived in 1804, it was nothing more than the decaying remnant of an abandoned village. Their guide informed them that the inhabitants had moved further up the river and joined forces with the Hidatsa.

The Discovery Corps continued their journey up river. A few days later, they encountered a large settlement where the Knife River joins the Missouri. After a week with this friendly, accommodating group of Native Americans, the Captains decided to make their winter camp nearby.

Kate and Mac followed the explorers north to the Fort Mandan replica near the site where the Corps had spent the winter of 1804 – 1805. It was a crude log structure with a high wall surrounding a few rectangular buildings. The living quarters had been divided into apartments for the men of the Corps. Each of the captains had his own room. Other buildings were used as storage rooms. The center of the fort was an open courtyard.

The winter months from November 1804 to April 1805 were brutal. Still, the men built their fort in less than a month and prepared for the next leg of their journey. One of the key accomplishments was enlisting French trapper Pierre Charbonneau, who brought along his wife, Sacagawea. According to one story, Lewis hired Charbonneau because he believed the Shoshone woman would be helpful in dealings with the Indians.

Mac and Kate got back to their camper in time for dinner. They decided to spend the night at a nearby RV park. They ate at a picnic table and went back into their mobile home to plan for the next leg of the trip. Great Falls, Montana, was the target. That meant covering between 300 and 350 miles each of the next two days. Kate needed a couple of tries to settle on Fort Peck as a good layover. She made a reservation at Fort Peck Marina and RV Park. Then she added stops at Crow Flies High Butte and Cut Bluff.

18

————

The morning began with the usual routines and a leisurely breakfast. Kate drove north on I-83. Around noon they stopped at Crow Flies High Butte. After a light lunch, they strolled around the park, taking in the view from the overlook. Lake Sakakawea, one of the largest reservoirs in the United States, stretched for miles in every direction. It covered the bottomlands where the Discovery Corps had camped both on their way west in 1805 and on their way home in 1806.

They continued north on ND-1804 following the Missouri River to Williston. They stopped to check out Cut Bluff before entering the city. Lewis climbed to that vantage point on April 22, 1805, and found a remarkable scene: "… immense herds of buffalo, elk, deer and antelope feeding in one common and boundless pasture."

They stopped in Williston for gas. Mac filled the tank while Kate picked up supplies.

Back in the camper, Kate helped Mac get settled and then set his computer in his lap. It was time for something new. The tale of Hondo Lane had run its course. Angie Lowe had dumped him for killing her husband, then changed her mind as he was about to ride off into the sunset. Chief Vittorio had led his band of Apaches on the warpath. The Calvary had charged out to rescue settlers and suffered a crushing defeat at the hands of the Apaches. The battered Calvary had collected settlers like Angie, Johnny and Hondo as they retreated to their fort. The Apaches had caught them for a final showdown. Hondo had taken command and led a successful stand. Angie and Johnny were ready to resettle in California with Hondo. A happy ending for the two lovers who were meant to be.

The display on Mac's computer screen looked like a word processor with a few extra sections. A big green circle with a microphone icon sat dead center on a toolbar floating at the top of the screen. Mac frowned as he studied the display. "Wha's this?"

:What is this: scrolled across the screen.

He glared at Kate. A stoic expression gave no hint of his inner turmoil, but she saw dismay when her eyes met his. She smiled sympathetically and took his face in her hands. She kissed him. "You're having trouble making yourself understood. We have to work on that."

Kate kissed him again and said, "This is *MyStory*, a speech-to-text storytelling app."

:This is my story a speech to text storytelling application: popped up on the screen.

She looked over and nodded. "The mic is picking me up."

The text on the screen read :The Mike is picking me up:

She touched the microphone icon. The circle turned red.

Mac asked, "Whuz goin' on?"

"Speech therapy. We're going to work on vocalization." She winked. "And I want to know all about you. We can kill both birds with one exercise."

"You awready know ev'rythin' worth knowin'." He heaved a sigh. "Da res' is borin'."

Kate took a headset from her neck and fitted it over Mac's head. The speaker covered his right ear. The mic projected to the corner of his mouth. "You'll need this to block out my voice and other noise."

She touched the red button. It turned green. She started the RV and maneuvered out onto the highway. "Tell me about yourself."

They were on ND-1804 following the Missouri River west. As they drove out of the city toward North Dakota's rolling plains, they passed acres of drilling rigs. An oil boom was fueling explosive growth in the local economy.

"I'mma retire' engineer wi' kids 'n' grannkids."

"When did you retire?"

"Twenny seventeen."

"Why?"

"I gah tiredda BS."

"How long did it take you to get to that point?"

"Abou' forddy years."

"I mean, how long were you thinking about retiring before you made the decision to do it?"

"I's in charge uh ver'f'cation. They 'signe' keystone cops to wri' procedures. Mess ennup on my des'. I hadda clean up. One day ligh' dawn'. Time to retire."

Mac turned to Kate. "Kepp me aroun' eight months."

"You must have been important."

"I's suppos' t' fin' our 'stakes 'fore cussomer. Dey didn' wan' cussomer complainin'."

Kate glanced over at the screen. "Not bad. I can clean it up."

"Whuz da poin'?"

"I want to figure out what we need to work on." She smiled. "And I want to post your story online."

"Wanna bore people t' death?"

She half-turned, flashing a mischievous grin. "There are websites that specialize in stories by elderly people. They get a lot of interest. Besides, I know your life wasn't that dull."

Mac shook his head. "Nah for me. Nobody else wannsa hear aboud it."

Kate shrugged. "Try me."

Mac closed his eyes and shook his head. The pause was too long. Kate was getting ready to give him a nudge when he said, "I start' on da groun' floor. Da Tech Rev'lushun was jus' beginnin'. We use' slide rules. Pock't calc'lators came later. Couldn'afford 'em. Very hard ta git cumput'r time." He studied the screen and shook his head. He took a deep breath and let it out. "Programmin' languages were prim'tive. I star' wi' machine language." He paused for another breath. "When I gah back from d'army, we use' FORTRAN." He looked up. Smiled. Nodded. "Later, I work' wi' all kinds of languages. Never could ge' Java." He looked over at Kate and shook his head. "I move' to tessin'. Couldn' keep up wi' d'velopments."

Kate looked at him out of the corner of her eye and nodded. Mac continued, "Firs' syssem I work' on had twenny eight compon'n's in big cab'nets. Seven fee' high 'n' two fee' wide." He looked up and gave his head a dismal shake. "I help' install some. Two weeks to get one runnin'." He turned to Kate. "It was moth-ball'. Dey foun' out a minicomput'r could do da job." He cackled. "Cellphone coul' do it now."

"I can see where that would be disappointing," Kate said.

Mac turned to her with an awkward attempt at a grin. "Daz da way i' works. I join' startup t' do sumpin excitin'. Company fold'. I was outta work but gotta contrac' consultin' wi' Motorola on Iridium."

Kate glanced over. "What's that?"

"Sevenny seven satellites. Coul' call any place on da planet. Goo' idea bu' technology move' too fas'. Dey sol' it to da gover'men' fer ten cents on da dollar. I try temp work. FAA contrac' for new communication syssem. Y two K wuzza nigh'mare. We didn' know how to keep airlines runnin' affer nineteen ninny nine. Dey needda plan. We were workin' on it. Bu' somebody else solve' da problem."

Mac looked at Kate and cackled. "Our stuff was scrapp'."

Her head jerked around to face him. "Scrapped? As in trashed."

"Yeah. I couldda stay' home 'n' watch TV."

"Was Y2K really a problem?"

"I'm tiredda talkin'. Can we lissen to a book?"

"Say, 'save file.'" Mac obeyed.

"Now 'mic off.'" Mac did as instructed. The green microphone circle turned red. Kate said, "You can take off the headset. We'll go over the file this evening." She looked over at Mac and flashed a grin. "I've got a book I want to listen to. It's an Alaskan adventure."

Mac shrugged. Kate said, "A Baltimore cop takes a job as police chief in a very small town in the rugged wilds of Alaska. He finds romance and discovers a murder mystery that needs his attention. I think it will be entertaining."

Mac nodded. "Sounns goo'. Le's hear it."

Kate grabbed her tablet with her right while she steered with her left. As she set up the book to play on their audio system, Mac observed, "D'stract'd drivin'."

Kate grimaced but ignored him. He said, "You ha' dis plan'."

She smirked. "I made some preparations."

The story opened with an anonymous man making a journal entry about his adventure climbing a mountain in Alaska. Then ex Baltimore cop Nate Burke flew into Lunacy, Alaska, to take over as police chief. For the next couple of hours, Kate drove along ND-1804 which merged into US-2 at Bainville, Montana. When she got to Nashua, she turned south on Duck Creek Road, which took them to the

Fort Peck RV Park on the shores of Lake Fort Peck - another reservoir created by a dam in the 1930s. The audio system kept them entertained with the story of Nate Burke getting a tour of Lunacy and meeting its citizens.

Discussions of the next day's drive began during dinner. Mac had decided he was going to see the Upper Missouri River Breaks. The spectacular panorama was rated as a "must see" in guide books. He wanted to see the bluffs from a boat on a three-day trip up the river. Kate said, "You are in no condition for an overnight camping trip."

"I'd juz be ridin' inna boa'."

"You'd have to get in and out of the boat and sleep on the ground."

"I slep' on da groun' before."

"But this time, you need a cane to get around and you're just learning how to do that."

Mac glared at her, but the wheels were turning in his head. He clamped his lips together and shook his head. Kate said, "Can I take that as a 'yes'?"

She grabbed her tablet and picked up Mac's travel guide. After a few minutes, she said, "There's a road that goes through the Judith Landing Campground. That's on the west end of the Upper Missouri River Breaks. Will that do?"

Mac leaned back and arched his brows. "I spose."

Kate played with Google Maps on her tablet. "We can do that but it will be a long drive – over 400 miles."

She did the dishes and poured some scotch. Then she pulled up the audio files Mac had recorded earlier.

He wasn't in a cooperative mood, but he helped clean up his answers. He balked when she tried to get him to practice some of the words. Kate said, "Com'on Mac. You need to retrain your muscles so people can understand you."

She wanted 20 minutes. He gave her 10.

19

They hustled through their morning routines. The day's drive would take over eight hours and Kate wanted to reach Great Falls by dinnertime. She had made reservations at the KOA camp near Malmstrom Air Base. She positioned Mac's headset and set his computer in his lap before shoving off. He glared. She grinned and winked.

As soon as they were rolling, Kate asked, "Was Y2K really a problem? The catastrophe never materialized." Mac looked at her with a wicked grin. "Poof. Solution 'pear' outta nowhere."

Kate turned to him with arched brows. He said, "I know people say 'twas nuttin'."

He shook his head. "We were tole it'd be da endda da worl'." He took a deep breath and sighed. "Sump'n hadda be done. It hadda work for computers runnin' differen' op'ratin' syssems. Millions of'm." Another deep breath. "Nobody in charge. Y two K was gonna be a 'saster."

Kate turned and met Mac's eyes. "But it wasn't."

"Couldda been." He took a deep breath. "Bu', alls well dat enns well."

Kate turned her attention to the road. She perked up and looked at him. "How did you get started in engineering?"

He shook his head. "Save file. Mic off. I'm tire'. Lez lissen to da story."

For the next two hours, they watched the scenery roll by as they listened. It was New Year's. Nate Burke was settling in and women were pursuing him. Three young men stranded on a mountain started the story in a new direction.

Kate stopped for gas on the outskirts of Chinook. Fifteen minutes later, she got them back on the road heading for Judith Landing Campground. They circled around Fort Belknap Reservation and Baldy Mountain. It took them an hour to reach Big Sandy, where they turned south on 236. It took another hour to get to Judith Landing. The last half hour on gravel.

Meanwhile, in Alaska, Sheriff Burke rescued the hikers and learned of a body in a cave on the mountain. It turned out to be his girlfriend's long-lost father. She wanted the ex-Baltimore police investigator to find the killer.

Mac and Kate had been sitting in the camper for four hours. They would need another four to get to Great Falls. She insisted they get out and walk around.

Judith Landing was not much to look at. It took them 20 minutes to tour the campground which consisted of a few campsites with picnic tables and fire rings and a ramp to accommodate boats. A small country store was open for business. The Bureau of Land Management provided a ranger station and outdoor toilets. Their literature gave a history of the site: in 1805, Lewis and Clark stopped there. In 1844, it became a trading post, and the Power and Newton cattle ranch, the largest ranch in Montana, was established. In 1855, Ferdinand Hayden discovered the first dinosaur fossils, and from 1880 to 1908, it was the base of a cable ferry operation.

As couple finished their tour, Mac tapped Kate on the arm and pointed excitedly when some kayakers pulled up to the boat ramp. "I've never been in a kayak," she snapped, "and I'm not going to try it now." Mac sneered and shook his head. She scoffed, "We'd probably drown."

They were able to view a little of the amazing cliffs but it was not the same as rafting down the river. Mac got to see a little more when Kate stopped halfway across the bridge. She only allowed him a quick look before continuing to the other side. Then they were back on gravel road as far as Winifred, where they picked up a real highway for the drive to Lewistown.

Kate said, "Before I restart the story, I want to know how you got started in engineering?"

Mac turned to stare at her. She kept her eyes on the road. He said, "We're nah recordin'."

"That's okay. I'll remember and we can go over it tonight."

He bit on his lower lip. "I'z an ignoran' kid. It look' like a goo' career 'n' I had qualifications."

"Such as?"

"I was goo' in math 'n' science." He took a deep breath. "I graduate' wi' honors."

"High school. Right?" She glanced over at him. "Where'd you go to school?"

"Roxborough." Mac looked up at the ceiling and shook his head as memories flooded back. "Neighborhoo' schoo'."

"College?"

"Univers'ty of Pennsylvania."

"Why?"

"I coul' affor' it."

"Did you want to go somewhere else?"

"No nee'. Goo' school 'n' price was righ'."

"You could have borrowed money."

"Nah. You don' borrow money ef you don' needda."

"Was it hard to find a job?"

"Nah." Mac paused to stare out the window at the scenery. "Engineerin' degree guarantee' job."

Kate said, "You got a job offer in May and proposed to Anne. When did you get married?"

"Lez liss'n to da story."

A suspicious suicide brought the State Police in to take over the investigation. Burke vowed to continue on his own.

Kate stopped in Lewistown to refuel. They got out, stretched their legs and bought coffee. When Mac was settled, Kate put his laptop in front of him and positioned the headset so he could dictate. She kissed him on the forehead and gave him a hug. "This is great. I want to hear more."

He scrunched his nose and shook his head. But he didn't try to take the headset off. Kate started the camper and got back on the road.

"So, you had a job waiting when you graduated. When did you marry Anne?"

"Endda June."

"Big wedding?"

"Jus' fammly."

"Just family?"

"It was tha' or big weddin'. We didn' wan' big."

"How did you break the news?"

"Wen' ta her parenns. She tole 'em 'n' we talk.'" Mac shook his head. "Wen' ta my parenns. Dad razz' Anne abou' bein' a Cam'b'll. Brough' up feu' b'tween M'Gregorz 'n' Cam'b'llz." He grimaced and shook his head, then smiled at Kate. "Anne tole 'im," he sucked in a breath, "Gregor M'Gregor marrie' Marion Cam'b'll. 'n' they were happy."

"What were your parents like?"

"Or'nary people." Mac closed his eyes and looked up at the ceiling. "Dad was manager a' da shipyar'. Mom taugh' gray schoo'."

Kate looked over. Smiled. Nodded. "Keep going."

"Dad dropp' outta high schoo' t'wor' a' da shipyar'. Di' dat 'til he retire'. Work' his way up da ranks." Mac took a deep breath and closed his eyes for a moment. "Mom taugh' little kids. She did lotta thin's bu' dat was her jo'."

"Did she have a degree?"

"High schoo'." Mac paused to think. "'n' teachin' certificate."

"Did you have a big house?"

"Apar'men' in Roxborough. Close to shipyar' 'n' schools."

"Three of you in an apartment? Must've been cramped."

"Four. Mom, Dad, sisser 'n' me."

Kate's mouth formed a silent "Oh."

"Daz all we knew. Frenns live' in doze apar'men's."

"What did you do for fun?"

"Stuff. Save file. Mic off. I'm bush'."

She grimaced and nodded. "I guess that's enough for now."

They hadn't gotten far. Near Hobson. A little past Moore. Two more hours to Great Falls. Kate glanced at a satellite view. Montana reminded her of an old woman. Strong and proud. Face furrowed from a lifetime of care and struggle. They crossed long stretches of arid, treeless plain followed by streams and mountain crests covered with trees.

The arrival of Spring in Alaska brought changes in Burke's life and in the life of his town. Some of the goings-on were violent. Many raised suspicions in the Sherriff's mind. His relationship with his girlfriend heated up. His investigation dragged on.

Kate got them set up in their campsite for the night. They listened to romantic music while they ate their dinner and relaxed. Then they worked on the memoir and speech therapy. He was asleep by the time she was ready to call it a night. She crawled into bed and clutched him against her naked body as if her love could pull him back from the grave.

20

Kate rousted Mac earlier than he would've liked. He sat up, dangling his feet over the edge of the bed, and glared to show his disapproval. She grinned. "We talked about making it to Missoula today. I checked that out last night. The museum will probably be closed by the time we get there. I went ahead and made reservations at an RV site."

That didn't seem to help. "Whadda ya mean?"

"It's three hours from here to the Missouri Headwaters State Park. Another three to Missoula." She pursed her lips as she gauged his reaction. Nothing. He listened but didn't respond. She said, "If we spend an hour at the Interpretive Center in Great Falls and an hour at the Headwaters Park," she shrugged, "we'll get to Missoula around five."

Mac blinked. "Bu' we coul' make it ba four."

Kate nodded.

"Le's ge' goin'."

She smiled. "The Interpretive Center doesn't open until nine."

While they were eating breakfast, Kate ventured, "We should go straight to Fairbanks from here."

Mac set his fork down and glowered. "Nah," he rasped.

"We've seen everything there is to see, and we can save hundreds of miles."

"We talk' abou' dis." He took a breath. "You 'gree' we stick ta da plan."

"You've been disappointed at every stop. What makes you think that will change?"

"Nuttin. Bu' I always finish whad I star'."

"Even if it means not making it to meet your cousin in Fairbanks?"

Mac grumbled, "Outta ma hanns."

Kate closed her eyes and shook her head. "Mac."

He scooped egg onto his toast and bit off a chunk. He studied Kate as he chewed. "E'er see da Rockies?"

She shook her head. "No."

"Spectac'lar. You needda see 'em."

"That's not important right now. I've got time."

"We all gah time." Mac took a breath. "'Til we don'." He reached over and squeezed her hand. "We're here now." Another deep breath. "We follow da Trail to da ocean." He shook her hand. "Jus' a coupla days."

Kate winced. "It's another thousand miles. And we'll be no closer to your cousin when we get there."

He gave her hand a reassuring squeeze. "You' be gla' we did it."

The Missouri River's Great Falls are a gift from the ice ages, but they were a nightmare for the Discovery

Corps. Lewis and Clark spent a month getting their equipment past the series of five falls.

According to some geologists, the river originally ran northeast to the Hudson Bay. Successive ice ages created glaciers that pushed down into the northern United States and blocked the channel. Water backed up, forming lakes that spilled into a new channel flowing southeast from Montana to St. Louis. The rechanneled river has supported plants, animals, red men, and white men for centuries.

The Lewis and Clark Interpretive Center looked like a long one-story building from the parking lot. Inside it was spacious and inviting. Self-guided tours took visitors through the exhibits. Mac spent his time on a display that told the story from the competing perspectives of the Discovery Corps and Native Americans. He nodded in agreement as he made his way through the version that chided the Captains for missing opportunities.

The rear of the museum overlooked the Missouri. A two-story diorama on the back wall depicted the Discovery Corps' struggle to get their equipment over the falls. Near the base of the tableau, a door opened out to a walkway that led to a trail running along the river's edge. Kate and Mac walked as far as the shore. From that vantage point, they could see that the Interpretive Center had been built into the cliffs along the river's banks.

They were in and out in half an hour. Kate got Mac set up for dictation and took off for the Missouri

Headwaters State Park. The day was pleasant. The mountains grand. And Mac was cooperative.

As soon as they were out of Great Falls heading south on I-15, Kate said, "Did you start working right after graduation?"

"Munny affer July 4."

"Did Anne have a job?"

"Programmer."

"Was that her major?"

"Psych." Mac shook his head. "She's in ma FOR-TRAN class." He turned to Kate and grinned. "She quit affer Junior came. Stay' home."

"When was that?"

"Cuppla years. 73. Affer we fix' our finances."

"What about Ann?"

"77."

"What were they like?"

"Smart. Reg'l'r kids." Mac paused. He took a breath. "Dey were hers. I's busy workin'."

Kate chuckled. "Just dumped them on her."

"Anne knew how ta gedda job. If she wanna work, she wouldda." Mac shook his head. "She work' in da library. Volunteer' when she want'."

Kate nodded. "What do you mean they were smart?"

"Toppa da class."

"What did they study?"

"Junior studie' 'lectric'l eng'neerin'. Godda MBA." Mac took another breath. "Ann studie' business. Gah her MBA too."

"What are they doing now?"

"Dunno. Dey talk' to dere mom."

"How about sports?"

"Junior play' foo'ball 'n' basketball. Ann play' basketball." Mac paused for a breath. "Did sumpen wi' horses. Had her own for a while."

Kate took a while to consider her next question. "How did things change after Junior and Ann moved out?"

Mac shrugged. "Nah much. She was busy 'n' I was busy. Save file. Mic Off." Mac turned to look at Kate. "Lez lissen ta da story."

Sheriff Burke continued his investigations. Some residents began to come up with recollections from the time his girlfriend's father disappeared. Nothing he could act on. The town council was divided over keeping him around. His romance was blossoming and he knew he wanted to stay.

Kate stopped at an overlook just outside of Three Forks, where they could see the three rivers running together to form the Missouri. They ate sandwiches and drank coffee while taking in the view. Then they pulled into the main parking lot of the Missouri Headwaters State Park.

Mac couldn't do much, so they walked around checking out interpretive displays. One explained the significance of the territory over the centuries. It had been an important hunting ground and a place to make camp for travelers crossing through the mountains. Sacagawea had grown up in that locale. She was camping near Three Forks with her family when a Hidatsa war party attacked and took her captive.

Back on the road, Kate asked, "What was it like when you and Anne were first married?"

Mac scowled at her, then looked back at the road. "We lef' Philadelphia. Bought a house in Jersey." He took a deep breath and let it out slowly. "Junior was born a year later. Ann came along a couppla years affer dat." He turned to Kate. "Anne stopp' workin' to stay home."

Kate waited a few seconds. "And?"

"Normal stuff. I's busy workin' on projects. Kids grew up 'n' wen' ta schoo'."

"What about your significant other?"

"I tole you. She stay' home."

"That's it? She just stayed home?"

"Belong' to clubs. Volunteer." Mac watched the scenery roll by. "I's assigne' to a project at NASA." He took a breath and let it out slowly. "We move' to Greenbelt." He smiled. "Nice place. Fam'ly friennly." He cackled. "It was a community plann' by our gover'men' 'n' it actually work'."

"I read about that. It was made a National Historic Landmark in 1997."

"Da's da place." Mac took a breath and let it out. "We stay' dere twenny years. Kids wen' ta high schoo' 'n' college."

"And they graduated at the top of their class?"

"Near da top." Mac took a breath. "Junior was in Science 'n' Engineerin' Magnet Program. Very brigh' kids."

"And Ann?"

He shook his head. "She wasn' da' smar'."

Kate's head snapped around. "Wow."

"Well. She wasn'." Mac took a deep breath and let it out slowly. "She's smar' enough but she couldn' do math worth a damn."

"What does that mean?"

Mac shook his head. "Lez lissen ta da story."

"Did you belittle your daughter?"

He glared at Kate. "Don' pu' words in ma mouth."

"So how did it work?"

He grimaced. "We steer' her into sompin practical." He took a deep breath and let it out slowly. "She wanna take da general curric'lum. We encourag' her ta take da Business Major."

Kate rolled her eyes and shook her head. She turned on the story.

Burke's girlfriend's mother had her own romantic troubles. An attempt was made on the sheriff's life. The investigation was shaking things up around the town.

Kate went straight to the Historical Museum at Fort Missoula. They reached the parking lot a little after four.

She asked, "Do you really want to spend the next hour checking out another fort?"

"Nah." Mac grimaced and shook his head. "Bu' I do wanna see what dey gah ta offer."

Buildings from the original fort and an extensive collection of artifacts gave a good idea of life in the nineteenth century. Displays inside the Historical Museum gave Mac what he really wanted. Early trade with European settlers provided Indigenous

Americans on the east coast with superior weapons and horses. It also pushed them to look for fresh hunting grounds where they could find more furs to trade. The Shoshone and Blackfeet invaded Three Forks, the traditional domain of the Salish or Flathead tribe. European explorers and trappers moved into the region in the nineteenth century. In 1841 the Jesuits established a mission there. They taught the Salish farming techniques. They built grist mills and sawmills. But when the Jesuits extended their mission to the despised Blackfeet, the Salish wanted nothing more to do with them.

Missoula began as a trading post. It became a town in 1866. The fort was built in 1877. Eventually it was manned by the all-black 25th Regiment. This created the strange arrangement of black soldiers protecting white settlers from displaced red men. The railroad reached Missoula in 1883, cementing the town's position as the most important settlement in Montana.

Over 2000 Japanese-Americans and Italian-Americans were held at the fort during the World War II internment.

21

Mac woke at three and made his way to the bathroom. Couldn't sleep. Poured a couple of fingers of whiskey. And sat in the captain's chair. He liked being in the driver's seat, even if he couldn't drive.

Kate came forward and put her arms around him. She wedged a breast against his cheek and kissed him on the forehead. "You okay?"

"Jus' thinkin'."

"About?"

"When Junior was a year ol', we too' a trip to Acadia Nation'l Par'." He held the whiskey up. "Use' ol' Chevy wagon aza cammer. Coul' sleep in da back whe' da sea' was down."

Kate sipped the whiskey and returned the cup. "Do you want to talk about it?"

"He's playin'. Los' his balance 'n' split his li'." Mac shook his head. "Hadda rush him to da clinic. Bu' firs', hadda raise da middle sea' 'n' pu' stuff in da back." He paused for a breath. Kate asked, "Why did you have to put the seat up?"

He scowled at her. Then he looked up at the ceiling. "He needda car sea'." Mac smirked, "By da time we gah to da clinic, bleedin' stopp'." He shrugged. "We check' inna motel for da nigh'."

"Bummer."

"Sometime thin's jus' don' work ou'."

Kate chuckled. Mac reached up and pulled her down for a kiss. Her lips pressed against his. She made a smacking sound as she pulled back. He said, "Go ba' ta be'. I'll be der inna bi'."

Breakfast was quiet. Kate broke the silence. "What's your cousin's name?"

Mac looked up and thought for a moment. "Kirss'n." He grinned. "Kirss'n Learned."

"When does she expect us?"

He shrugged. She pressed her lips into a disappointed frown and shook her head. "You haven't talked to her."

"I'll sen' email."

After breakfast, they headed south on US-93. At Lolo, they turned west on US-12, which took them through the Nez Perce National Forest. They drove for hours along the Lochsa River with rugged peaks towering over them.

Kate asked, "What was the best decision you ever made?"

He countered, "Tell me sumpin abou' Kath'rin Gra'am."

She snickered. "You first."

He snorted and growled, "Marryin' Anne."

"And the worst?"

"I can' say my 'cisions were goo' or ba'." Mac took a deep breath and let it out slowly. "Sometime' I jus' did wha' hadda be done. Sometime'," he looked over at Kate, "I too' chance. Dinn' always work ou'. Bu' I wouldn' say I made ba' 'cisions."

Kate looked at him with arched brows. Mac shrugged. "I lef' a goo' job to join a frien' atta startup. Look' promisin'. We broke new groun' 'n' 'complishe' amazin' thin's. Bu' company fold' affer two years." Mac shook his head and took another breath. "Nex' four years I work' tem' jobs. Den I godda job wi' da bes' company I ever work for."

Kate rocked her head. "What's the takeaway? Sometimes a bad decision works out in the long run?"

Mac watched the scenery roll by. "Woul' you've come on dis tri' if you knew we'd en' u' like dis?"

She sighed. "Probably. You needed help. It was an opportunity to travel."

"For a hunner dollars a day?"

She laughed. "Again, I'm not doing this for the money."

"Why are ya doin' i'?"

"Adventure. Besides I like you."

Mac closed his eyes and nodded. "So, you unner-stan' why I leffa good jo' to work atta starrup."

Kate turned on the story. Bait left by a mysterious villain brought on a bear attack that threatened Burke, his girlfriend, Meg, and her dogs. Meg grabbed her rifle and killed the bear. More clues emerged. Meg's father had won money in a poker game the night before he began that last, fatal mountain climb, and a lost piece of jewelry was found at the crime scene. Nate burke bought a ring and proposed. Meg agreed to marry him.

Kate stopped for lunch at the US 12 Lenore Rest Area. She and Mac got out for a short walk. When they were back on the road, Mac asked, "You gonna tell me abou' yer life?"

She grimaced and shook her head. "Not right now."

She turned on the story. The clues finally fell into place. They knew who killed Meg's father. They cornered him at the May Day celebration being held in town. Burke arrested him, and married his sweetheart.

Kate pushed on to an RV park south of Hermiston, Oregon. They had been on the road eight hours. It was time for dinner. It would take them less than a day to reach Fort Clatsop and the Pacific Ocean. As she helped Mac out of his seat, she pressed her cheek against his and whispered, "I'll tell you about it tomorrow."

22

Mac and Kate had decided on a break at Stevenson, Washington, about halfway to Fort Clatsop. They ate a leisurely breakfast before hitting the road. Twenty minutes later, I-84 swung left to follow the river. They continued through Boardman, a small farming town, and entered a gorge with steep banks towering over them on either side. Kate picked this setting to begin her story. "Your life wasn't boring, Mac. Mine was."

She drove in silence for a few more minutes. "My life story is a tale of talent wasted." She kept her eyes focused straight ahead. "That's egotistical. But I have the brains and the talent to be somebody." She turned to Mac with a glum expression. "You know how that worked out."

He watched and waited. She seemed focused on the mountains beyond the high ridges lining the river. "I was a nerd. I loved science." She grinned at him. "I loved cutting up arthropods and frogs."

"Wha' happen'?"

"I discovered boys." She pursed her lips and shook her head. "And I liked them more than science."

"Tha's it? Books 'n' boys?" Mac cringed. "What abou' other stuff?"

"I played basketball."

"Das good."

"I was a benchwarmer."

"Jus' one seas'n?"

"I stuck it out through high school. There were social benefits."

Mac shook his head disapprovingly. A smile played across Kate's face. "I found my niche in tennis. I could cover the court and I had a wicked serve."

"Li' Sally Ride."

"She was better than me."

"Why aren' you a dock'r?"

"I didn't keep my grades up."

"Why nah?"

"Too busy chasin' boys."

She peeked sideways to catch his reaction. He closed his eyes and shook his head. "Izat how you end' up in da hospital?"

Kate shot a glare in his direction. Mac turned his attention to the scenery across the river. A deep, melodic voice on the audio system announced the beginning of a new chapter in *Stormy Seas*.

Kate stopped the story when she had parked in front of the Columbia Gorge Interpretive Center. Inside, exhibits covered millions of years of geological development, thirteen thousand years of Native

American occupation, and developments following the influx of European settlers.

The story began with the North American plate pulling away from the supercontinent Pangea and sliding northwest into the ocean. It was a rough ride that pushed boulders up through the surface, creating a mountainous belt running from Canada into Mexico. The North American plate slid up onto the Farallon plate when the two landmasses collided. Islands on the Farallon plate merged with the western edge of North America to form its Pacific Coast.

Ten million years later, volcanic activity created the Cascade Mountains. Mount Rainier, the highest mountain in the range, is still an active volcano. Glaciers sliding down from Canada scraped away sediment, leaving bare rock. Rivers created as the glaciers melted further eroded the mountains and carried topsoil to the lowlands.

At the end of the last Ice Age, Lake Missoula, a body of water as large as Lake Erie and Lake Huron combined, covered much of Montana. Eventually, the ice wall holding all that water gave way sending a flash flood many times the size of the Amazon River hurtling toward the Pacific. The effect was to carve a four-thousand-foot-deep canyon through the mountains. When the convulsions had died down, the Columbia River was the only navigable passageway through the Cascades to the ocean.

Early human settlements began appearing along the Columbia River near the rapids now known as The Dalles. The inhabitants fished, hunted and traded for over ten thousand years before European settlers arrived.

An hour of wandering through the exhibits in the museum improved Kate's mood. When they were back on the road in open country, she picked up her tale. "A mutual friend introduced me to Mark at a party. He was a grown-up version of the guys I had dated in high school. Charming, witty, and good-looking. The problems were harder to spot."

Lush, green mountains sped past as the RV rolled along the highway. Kate seemed caught up in the memory. "He sold used cars. That gave him plenty of opportunities to polish his act. You were his best friend as long as he got what he wanted." She looked over at Mac and smiled wanly. "I moved in with him. We had a great honeymoon until classes resumed in the fall. School was never hard for me. But I had a job, classes, and tons of homework. Our sex life suffered." She pursed her lips and rocked her head. "It pretty much died." She shrugged. "He started drinking. That brought out his childish, demanding side. I thought," Kate rocked her head, "I hoped we could hold out until semester break. He didn't see it that way. He started bullying me. Sometimes he was violent. One night he beat the shit out of me." Kate's head dropped. Her eyes closed. Her jaw clenched. Her head jerked violently and popped back up. She took a deep breath and blew it out. "I woke up in the hospital. I don't remember how I got there. I've been told a neighbor rescued me."

Fatherly advice ran through Mac's mind. He looked over at Kate but said nothing. She stared absently at the road ahead. Memories of the events held her attention. Fortunately driving is a subconscious process like breathing and walking. They were on the road to Fort Clatsop and some part of her mind was making sure they got there safely. She said, "My dad came to the hospital and told me I had to go visit cousin Jimmy for a while." She looked at Mac and grimaced. "Mark had come by the hospital. They wouldn't let him see me. He went to my parents and apologized. After that, they spotted him driving by the house once or twice a day. Dad decided he was dangerous."

She drifted off again. Then picked up. "He got me out of the hospital a day early and put me on a plane to St. Louis." She shrugged. "I'd never mentioned Jimmy to Mark so he wouldn't know where to look for me. But just to be safe, I used the name Jennifer Jones when I got to St. Louis." She sighed. "A 'while' became months. I found a job because I was bored. That's how I got started at St. Elizabeth's. I didn't know what to do about school, so I did nothing." She wiped the back of her hand across her cheeks. "Months became years and I settled in. I rented an apartment, got a used car, and went to work every day."

Kate lapsed into silence. They were nearing Portland. She rocked her head slightly from time to time. She said, "That's my life in a nutshell. I've been living and working in St. Louis for over 10 years and nothing stands out. Not a damn thing."

After they passed through Portland, Kate found an Oldies station to fill the silence.

At Fort Clatsop, a Park Ranger spotted the tall, stunning young woman escorting an elderly man as they were getting out of their camper. The geezer needed a cane. He wore a permanent sneer that suggested he had suffered a stroke. The Ranger decided he would have a one-on-one talk with the woman - just to see what would happen.

At the top of the hour, he shepherded the group from the visitor center to the Captain's quarters. He prowled across the room in front of the tourists taking time to focus on each one individually. He smiled a little when his eyes fell on Kate. She felt a warm glow but kept a straight face.

He began, "Congratulations. You have reached the end of the trail. That was the dilemma facing Meriwether Lewis at the end of November 1805. The Discovery Corps had started west in May 1804. They had crossed the Great Plains and the Rocky Mountains. When they reached the Pacific Coast, they had gone as far as they could. But Lewis couldn't stop. He owed President Jefferson a report." The Ranger paused to smile at the group. "Besides, he had a boatload of souvenirs to take back to Washington. He ordered a fort built and established military routines. The men of the Discovery Corps were given regular assignments. Guard duty became part of the daily regimen. That was the only way to keep them from running off to live with the natives."

He paced across the room one more time. He turned. "The men threw together the original version of Fort Clatsop in three weeks. They finished just before Christmas. It took modern men with modern technology 18 months to build a replica in 1955." He winked at Kate and smirked. "But they didn't need a roof to shelter them from cold winter rains."

He paused to survey the room. With a sweep of his hand, he told the group, "This building was used by Lewis, Clark, Toussaint Charbonneau, his wife Sacajawea and their two children. The other building was shared by the rest of the team."

He paced the room once more, collecting his thoughts. "The Discovery Corps had accomplished all of its major goals. They had explored the new Western territories that came with the Louisiana Purchase. They had followed the Missouri to its source and continued to the Pacific Ocean. They had made contact with indigenous peoples. And they had established their country's presence in the territory. That was important because the British, the French, and the Spanish had already established their presence and were eager to exploit the country's riches." He paused and surveyed the group. "The Columbia River marks the boundary between Oregon and Washington. Lewis and his team were conned into moving to the Oregon side by members of the Clatsop tribe. The elk would provide them with plenty of food for the winter. By the time the weather had improved enough for them to return East they were tired of the Clatsop and they never wanted to see another elk steak. Take your time looking around. I will be available to answer any questions you have."

He had focused on Kate during his talk. He had flirted with his eyes as the group broke up. She was flattered. He removed his hat, revealing curly, red hair as he eased over to introduce himself. The smile on his freckled face was engaging. The way he filled out his uniform convinced Kate he was her type. He said his name was Chris Jenkins and asked, "Where are you from?"

"St. Louis," Kate said brightly.

The conversation picked up from there. Mac moved over to a small table that was set up as Lewis's workspace. An open journal, quills and an ink jar sat on top as if the Captain had taken a break from making notes on the journey.

Chris was staring directly into Kate's eyes. She stared back, daring him to make a move. When nothing happened, she asked, "How did the Discovery Corps get hooked up with the Clatsop?"

Jenkins grinned. "They were related to Indians that the Discovery Corps dealt with at The Dalles."

"So, there was some sort of recommendation?"

"The two groups were in communication."

"That was handy."

He laughed. "Yes and no. The Clatsop helped the Discovery Corps locate its winter quarters and traded with them. But Lewis thought they were sneaky and thieving."

"Bummer."

"Lewis needed two canoes for the return trip. The Clatsop would only agree to give him one. He stole a second one on his way out."

Kate laughed. Mac said, "Don' we needda park da RV?"

Kate jumped. She turned to Mac and said, "Yep." She shook hands with Jenkins and said, "Thank you. It was a pleasure talking to you."

When they left the reconstructed Fort, Kate made reservations near Olympia and they took off.

23

An email from Kirsten Learned gave Mac a phone number. He called while Kate was making dinner. The conversation was friendly but short on details. He was in Olympia, Washington and would leave for Fairbanks in the morning. He would have to get back later after his plans had firmed up.

A sullen Kate picked at her dinner. Finally, she pushed her plate away and looked at Mac. The grim mask on her face barely concealing the hurt and disappointment. "Did I miss the part where you told your cousin you were bringing me along?"

"I was plannin' t' tell her nex' time."

"I see."

"You gonna Google da route?"

"I already did," she growled. "I want to take the ferry."

"Dere's a ferry to Fairbanks?"

She shook her head. Her lip curled into a sneer. "Fairbanks is inland. The ferry will take us from Bellingham to Haines. That will cut down on our driving."

Mac stood, scooped up the plates and took them to the sink. He started a pot of coffee. "How far to Fairbanks?"

"From here? 2300 miles. Google estimates 43 hours."

"An' da ferry?"

"3 hours to Bellingham. 72 hours on the ferry. 11 hours to Fairbanks."

"86 hours?" Mac shook his head. "Daz a lon' time."

"72 hours on the ferry is 3 days. 43 hours on the road is 6 to 8 days. The ferry will be faster."

"How much?"

"6 thousand."

"Yer jokin'," Mac grumped.

Kate went to the cabinet and took out a couple of cups. She put an arm around Mac's waist and gave him a peck on the cheek. "You wanted me to see the mountains. I want us to see the coast."

Mac shook his head. "Shit."

"Take it out of my pay."

"Daz sixxy days. Trip won' take dat lon'."

"Take it out of what you owe me."

"Den you gah no money."

"I'm going back to work." Kate was matter-of-fact. "What're you gonna do?"

Mac studied the ceiling. *How the fuck should I know?* He took her in his arms and kissed her. "You don' care abou' da money?"

She poured the coffee and took the cups to the table. "I care very much." She pulled her chair out and turned to face him. "I want to spend it on a cruise up the coast."

Mac took his seat and sipped his coffee. "Daz it? Daz all you wan'?"

She sat and looked into his eyes. "I want the camper."

"Da cammer? Why?"

"It's my home. It's us. Our kitchen. Our bed. Our shower."

He blew a puff of air out and brushed a hand through what was left of his hair. "Won' do me much goo' if yer nah aroun'."

"Come back to St. Louis with me."

"I dunno." Mac shook his head. "Haven' figure' out what I wanna do." He shut his eyes and blew out through his nose. "Don' know how much longer I gah."

He stood and walked to the sink. "I godda goal. Affer I see Kirssen, I gah nuttin."

"Do you love me, Mac?"

"Yeah."

"Come to St. Louis. We can take it one day at a time for as many days as we have left."

He drained his cup. Rinsed it. And set it in the sink. "So da ferry is da way ta go?"

She nodded. He said, "You ma' da reservation?"

Kate howled, "Mac!"

"You gah da details."

She conceded, "I have to call them by ten to confirm."

"Do dat." Mac studied her momentarily. "I tell Kirssen 'bouda week."

24

Kate got in touch with the Alaska Marine Highway System to finalize the reservations while they ate breakfast. Whittier came up. It was due south of Fairbanks. That would eliminate a detour into Canada. An extra day on the open waters of the Bering Strait would offer more exciting scenery. They could still get a room for two, but the agent recommended a stateroom with facilities because of Mac's condition. That would boost the fare to $8000. Mac rolled his eyes. "Migh'ez well. In fer a penny in fer a poun'."

Kate had to get them to the pier by eleven for boarding. They dropped everything and hit the road. An easy adjustment when you're traveling in a camper. The trip was supposed to take three hours. She got them to the boarding dock with time to spare, thanks to her lead foot.

The Bellingham Marine Terminal, where the Alaska Marine Highway ferries load and unload, sat across from a train terminal at the south end of a sprawling city. When Kate and Mac arrived, cars and

RVs were lined up and boarding. Pedestrians were walking up a gangplank to get on the ship.

Kate pulled up the ramp and into the gaping jaws of the giant vessel. Shadowy figures in fluorescent jackets waved flashlights, directing them toward a parking spot in the cavernous, dimly lit hold. Kate maneuvered the RV into position. The ferry's crew secured the vehicle while the couple packed clothes and necessities. The RV would be off-limits until they reached Whittier.

Their stateroom was on the third level, eight flights up from the noisy, foul-smelling parking bay. It was almost sumptuous. Four bunks, two dressers, and a round table with four chairs. A bathroom with a sink, a toilet, and a shower. And an amazing view.

They would share one of the beds, but they each got a dresser.

A laminated folder on the table provided information about the ship and the cruise. Continental breakfast was available from 6:30 until 11:30. Dinner was served between 5 and 7. Room service could be ordered until 11 p.m.

Their ship pulled away from the pier into Bellingham Bay around 4. It was scheduled to dock at Ketchikan at 6 in the morning after two nights and a day at sea.

That day was uneventful. Gossamer clouds dotted clear, blue skies. The Alaskan coast rolled past wild and beautiful. Eagles soared overhead. Whales and bears kept out of sight.

Kate established a routine. Exercise first thing, followed by breakfast and a stroll around the deck. They met a few more passengers headed for Whittier. Casual conversation with one couple, Ed and Edna Whitman, led to a discussion of Lewis and Clark, which progressed to a more general appraisal of US history. The Whitmans could talk all night about that subject. They were writers who specialized in historical novels. They were also avid bridge players who would spend hours teaching the game to Mac and Kate over the next few days.

In the early afternoon, a lecture on Ketchikan was given in the dining area. Once the group was settled, a uniformed man stepped to the front and center. "I'm Ranger Roy Rogers of the National Park Service. I'm on this cruise to provide you with information about Alaska, one of the world's great wilderness areas." He was a tall, ruggedly handsome man in his mid-forties. "Back in the middle of the last century, some men were sitting around a table in a bar in San Francisco. They began reminiscing about life back home. A Texan took over the conversation. He carried on about how big everything was where he came from. When he paused to take a breath, a gentleman from Alaska said, 'You should know we're going to cut Alaska in two. That will make Texas the third-biggest state.'"

He waited for the twitter to die down before continuing, "We are headed for Ketchikan. That's a mangled version of the Native American name for the place. It means 'Thundering wings of an eagle'."

"We are sailing past the Tongass National Forest, one of the largest national forests in the US. A big part of it is a temperate rain forest - one of the few remaining in the world. The Tongass also has mountains glaciers and fjords as well as a border with Canada. Wildlife is abundant and diverse. There are elk, moose, goats, bears, wolves, eagles, salmon and other fish. Some of the species are unique to this region."

"White men focused on lumber and salmon when they settled here. A boomtown grew up. Like other Wild West boom towns, it had a thriving red-light district. Creek Street was lined with brothels. Times have changed. Logging is no longer allowed. But many of the residents are employed in the commercial fishing industry. Now that tourism has become an important part of the economy, the bawdy houses have been converted to shops and restaurants. Dolly's House which was one of the most popular brothels is now a museum. Make sure to stop in and look around while you're in town."

"That's right. We've got a ten-hour layover scheduled. You'll have time for breakfast, lunch and sightseeing. You should spend some time at the Southeast Alaska Discovery Center and the Great Alaskan Lumberjack Show. The Totem Heritage Center and the Saxon Totem Park are a couple of places where you can check out Ketchikan's famous totems. There are number of rides and tours that you might find interesting. The Ketchikan Visitors Bureau located on the cruise ship dock has free maps to help you find your way around."

In the morning, Ed and Edna joined Mac and Kate at breakfast. They were Virginians who had met as professors teaching at the University of Alaska in Anchorage. Before they retired, he had taught American history while she taught business. Tall, gangly, and blue-eyed with a full head of white hair, Ed could have been a Dick Van Dyke impersonator. Edna looked more like Angela Lansbury.

"So now you just travel around?" Asked Kate.

"We write," Ed said. "I retired from teaching so I could concentrate on my writing."

"We do travel," Edna interjected. "We have to do our research."

"Gonna wri' sumpin aboud Alaska?" Mac asked.

"We're returning from a visit with our daughter and her family in San Diego," Edna explained. "What about you?"

Kate looked at Mac, waiting for him to answer. He took his time considering what to say. "We 'cided ta see da country."

The professors wanted more but let it drop. Edna asked, "What are your plans for today?"

"We haven't made any," Kate said.

"You're interested in history, Mac," Ed said. "You should at least visit the Southeast Alaska Discovery Center. Why don't you join us for little downtown sightseeing?"

"I dunno," Mac grumbled. "I migh' sit here 'n' people watch."

"I think you'll find the Discovery Center more interesting. You should check out Dolly's House." Ed urged with a mischievous grin. "I'd like to treat you to lunch at an establishment on Creek Street. I've always wanted to spend some time in a brothel."

Edna rolled her eyes. "He's not joking."

They agreed to get an Uber ride to the museum. After that, they would see how Mac felt.

The foursome took in the museum and Dolly's House, then lunched at a rehabilitated house of ill repute. When they got back to the ship, Mac needed a nap. He was back on deck to watch the chaos as a new group of passengers boarded for the trip to Juneau.

The ferry continued north on the inner passage, a series of channels between the coastal islands. A lecture on Juneau was given after dinner that evening. The Ranger bided his time at the front of the room while tourists got settled.

"My name is Roy Rogers. Yes, that really is my name. I'm not related to the cowboy who started a fast-food chain. My parents grew up on his movies and watched his TV series religiously. When I came along, they named their son after their hero."

"We will dock at Juneau, the capital of Alaska, around noon tomorrow. It's one-of-a-kind. It is the second largest city in the United States by land area. But with a population of only 35,000 it is Alaska's third largest city. Most of the land is uninhabitable. The city is bounded on the west by the Gastineau Channel and Douglas Island. Mountains with the Juneau Icefield and glaciers like the Mendenhall surround it on the other three sides. Juneau shares a border with Canada. It is the only state capital in the

United States that borders a foreign country. It is one of two state capitals that cannot be reached by road. People and goods are brought in by air or by water. Cruise ships bring a million visitors a year to see the sights."

Rogers paused to survey the crowd. "Some of you are wondering how Juneau could end up being the capital of Alaska." He paused. Took a couple of steps and turned back to his audience. "The answer is a four-letter word. Gold. In 1880, George Pilz offered a reward to anyone who could bring him a gold nugget. When he got one, he sent miners to find more. Richard Harris and Joe Juneau succeeded and the gold rush was on. They established a tent city. The settlement was originally called Harrisburg. Later the miners voted to change the name to Juneau. In 1906, Juneau emerged as the largest city in Alaska. The territorial government was relocated there because federal law required territorial legislatures to be seated in the largest city. So far, attempts to move the capital to Anchorage have been unsuccessful."

He paused again. "Our layover in Juneau will be too short for some of the sights. You won't be able to get to the Juneau Icefield and back. The Glacier Gardens Rainforest Adventure would probably take too long. But the Mount Roberts Tramway will give you some spectacular views of the area. Around town, the state capital building and the city museum have tours that will interest some of you. The Red Dog Saloon and the Alaskan Brewing Company are worth a visit. We'll dock near the Visitor's Center which has information about all the attractions. It also has maps to help you find your way around."

As soon as the ferry docked, Mac and Kate took off with the Whitman's for Mount Roberts. They stopped by the Red Dog Saloon for a long lunch and a couple of beers. When they returned to the ferry, Mac napped. Another Ranger talk was scheduled after dinner.

Once again, Rogers stood front and center, a rough-hewn man in a snappy Ranger uniform, biding his time as people filed into the room. When they were settled, he began, "I am Ranger Roy Rogers of the National Park Service. We're meeting early this evening because our ship is approaching one of the grand sights on this route. Glacier Bay." He took a couple of steps and turned back. Surveying the audience, he asked, "Did any of you have a run in with the frosties this afternoon?" He paused. "Frostitutes. That's what we call hookers up here." He watched the reaction and grinned. "I wouldn't admit it either."

He continued, "We are currently sailing around the north end of Admiralty Island into the Icy Channel. That will take us past Glacier Bay and out into the Gulf of Alaska. From there we will sail north along the coast to Yakutat. The Glacier Bay National Park and Preserve will be visible most of the night.

"It is spread over 3.3 million acres. The states of Delaware and Rhode Island could be crammed into it with a few nips and tucks. The park is five times the size of Washington DC but doesn't have a single politician. This is one of the world's great wildlife habitats. It's something like a big zoo except the animals feed themselves.

"Call it God's Zoo. Noah's Ark. The list of animals in Glacier Bay National Park and Preserve is a Who's Who of North American fauna. Its residents include bear, wolves, coyotes and foxes, lynx, moose, deer, mountain goats and sheep, porcupine, marmots, beaver. Bald eagles and golden eagles, falcons including the endangered peregrine falcon, hawks, owls, woodpeckers and ravens, and even hummingbirds are flying around. Along the coast, we have seals and sea lions, whales, dolphins, and sea otters. You won't be able to see much of that on this cruise. But the whales and the glaciers will be on display throughout the night."

He paced for a minute. "Humpback whales and gray whales have returned from their winter vacations down south. The orcas and porpoises are out there as always. The glaciers are thinning and receding." He chuckled. "They remind me of my father's hair. When he married Mom, his hair was thick. It tumbled over his ears and forehead. I think she married him because she liked running her fingers through that mop of fur. When I entered high school, it was thinning and he had developed a prominent forehead. By the time I finished college he had a widow's peak. The last time I saw him I said, 'Give up, Dad. Get your hair shaved off. Bald is in these days.'"

That got a few half-hearted chuckles. Rogers stopped to study his audience with a glum expression.

He shook his head. "They're going to have to spring for some canned laughter." That got a real laugh.

He picked up the thread, "The glaciers are still visible - at least some of them. There are over a thousand glaciers in the park. Some are tidal or tidewater glaciers. That means they've reached the shore and extend into the bay. They calve or shed icebergs into the water. You'll probably get to see some of that. Terrestrial glaciers are still sliding from the mountains to the sea. We'll make an announcement over the speaker system when the more famous glaciers come into view."

Rogers paused and turned. He took a few steps with his head down. Straightening his shoulders, he returned to the center and flashed a smile. "Tomorrow, we will be stopping over at Yakutat. That's a close approximation of the Tlingit name for the area. It means 'Place where the canoes rest.' It is a natural harbor at the north end of Alaska's Southern Panhandle. It was one of several settlements maintained by the Indigenous People before European settlers began to arrive. Toward the end of the 18th century, the Russia-America Company built a fort on the site to facilitate trade in sea otter pelts. At the end of the 19th century, ambitious European settlers were mining for gold. During World War II, the US Army Air Force built a base there. It is still used as an airport. Later on, Yakutat became the first Alaskan city with a surf shop. That earned it a spot in the sequel to the movie Endless Summer."

He grinned and nodded. "There is quite a bit to do in Yakutat. The Tlingit have a strong presence. Their traditions and artwork are on full display. The highest coastal mountain range in the world, the St. Elias Mountains, and the Hubbard Glacier provide a magnificent backdrop for the town."

He nodded and grinned again. "That should be enough to keep you busy for the next 24 hours."

The night was everything Ranger Roy Rogers had promised. The glaciers were spectacular. Whales and dolphins cavorted in the open waters of the Gulf. Seals, sea lions and otters were visible onshore or in the waters nearby.

In the morning, Mac announced that he was not up for a walk around the town. He was staying on the ferry. Kate insisted she would stay with him. The Whitmans took off to check out Yakutat's history and learn more about the Tlingit.

That evening the four of them ate a quick dinner and got up on deck to watch as their ship sailed past the Hubbard Glacier. It was crackling like a bonfire, except the crackles sounded like thunderclaps. The din built to a roar, and a block of ice the size of a house slid into the gulf, creating waves that rocked the giant ferry in spite of its load of cars and people. Edna remarked, "Now *THAT* makes this whole boat ride worthwhile."

She watched the action along the face of the glacier for several minutes before casually remarking, "I think we should spend the night playing bridge."

"Wha' aboudda ranger?" Mac demanded.

Edna turned and gave him a sad look. "I don't think I could sit there and listen to the man struggling to make Whittier sound interesting."

"Whittier *is* interesting," Ed countered.

"Because the whole town lives in one 60-year-old high-rise?"

"That's an exaggeration," Ed sneered. "Besides there's more to Whittier than Begich Towers."

"Right. They have a gravel runway that bush pilots call an airport."

"You're being rude," Ed scolded. He turned to Mac and Kate. "Whittier sits in a protected cove in Prince William Sound. It is a good jumping off point for journeys into the interior. The Chugach used to it for thousands of years. Miners looking for gold started their trek to the Yukon from what is now Whittier. Army engineers set up operations there during World War II. They built a port and a railroad spur that connected to the Alaska Railway. They also built a couple of high-rises to house their personnel. When they pulled out around 1960, the locals took over one of the buildings and renamed it Begich Towers. Cruise ships began using the port in the 70s and a highway was constructed to connect Whittier to Anchorage."

"And now it's a tourist trap," Edna quipped. "Let's go play bridge."

Ranger Roy Rogers noted that the old man and his hottie companion were not in the audience that night. Disappointing. But she was just one of the good-looking women on the cruise.

Plans for the next day came up during the bridge game. Kate said she would find a place to overnight near Anchorage. Edna told her to drive straight through to Fairbanks. Kate shook her head. "I want to get there in the middle of the day. I don't know my way around, and I've never met Mac's cousin."

"Wha' aboud you?" Mac asked.

"We'll get on a shuttle to Anchorage if possible. Otherwise, we'll take a cab."

"You don't have a car?" Kate asked.

"No. We flew out," Ed said. "Our car is at the airport in Anchorage."

Kate offered, "We can give you a ride."

Mac grimaced and Edna recoiled. "We don't want to impose."

Kate scowled at Mac. "It's no problem. We have plenty of room. And you can show us around Anchorage when we get there."

The issue was settled.

25

K ate got them back on their regular schedule of exercise and breakfast before taking on a day of driving. The trip to Fairbanks was a seven-hour drive through the rugged Matanuska-Sustina Valley and over the Alaska Range. They skirted the eastern edge of the Denali National Park and Preserve. The Chugach Mountains dominated the skyline on their right.

Once they reached the city, it took another half hour to find the Learneds' house, a modest ranch with a view of the Chena River.

Nobody was home. Mac called his cousin's cell. She directed them to a sports and adventure emporium on University Boulevard, a few minutes from her house.

Kirsten stepped out onto the sidewalk. She was looking for an elderly gentleman. An old cripple escorted by a two-bit whore hobbled toward her and said, "Kirssen, I'm yer cousin Dahnl' M'Gregor."

"Hi, Don. It's good to finally meet you in person." Her tone was less than welcoming. She skipped the pleasantries and invited them inside for a tour. Her barely concealed discomfort made Mac acutely conscious of his appearance and speech. He suddenly felt the left side of his face curling into a perpetual snarl. He was certain he had slurred his greeting despite Kate's therapy.

University Outfitters, the business Kirsten owned and operated with her husband, was set up for the sports and outdoor adventure crowd. It carried an impressive stock of wares -- sporting goods, camping gear, clothes, and miscellaneous tech stuff, all designed for college students and hip young professors. Nothing in the establishment interested Mac or Kate.

Kirsten turned the store over to an assistant for the rest of the day. Her husband, Bob, joined the group at the house and took them for a quick tour of the city. "We'll start with the university. It's close. Besides, that's where I work."

"What do you do?" Kate asked.

"I teach at the Geophysical Institute."

"He also heads a climate change research team for the UN," Kirsten threw in.

"Sounds exciting," Kate said.

"It is," Bob said without taking his eyes off the road. "It helps me keep up to date and provides material for some of my classes."

As they approached the campus, Bob said, "I understand you drove up from Anchorage today."

Kate said, "Yes. The ferry got us to Whittier yesterday afternoon. I didn't want to be driving in the dark, so we stopped over in Anchorage. A native would probably have driven up yesterday."

"It does take some getting used to," Bob observed. "I'd really love to show you around the campus. Our Museum of the North is one of the best in the world. Give me a call if you have time for an extended tour."

Mac nodded but said nothing. He had embarrassed himself enough for one day. Kate glared at him before answering, "That sounds wonderful. We could do it tomorrow or whenever it's convenient for you."

Bob drove them around the campus and took them downtown for a quick drive-by of the major tourist attractions. Mac was impressed. The professor was as good as any tour guide. He pointed out the sights, gave the historical background, and threw in juicy bits of lore. When he was wrapping up, he offered to take some time off and show them around. Kate looked at Mac. When he didn't respond, she said, "That sounds great, Bob. Could we talk about it tomorrow after we have gotten some rest?"

"Sure."

What else was the guy going to say?

They ended up at an Italian restaurant for dinner. Conversation was limited. Kirsten and Mac had spent decades hashing out their family history. Catching up on current events didn't take long. Her two children had graduated from college and worked for tech companies in California. Mac had only a vague understanding of what his children were up to. They weren't talking to him. That wasn't something he wanted to share with strangers over dinner.

Kirsten's husband regaled them with some stories of his field research in the Alaskan wilds. Kate reluctantly owned up to working part-time jobs. She gave out a version of her meeting Mac at a diner where she worked nights. "Nurse" and "nursing" were never mentioned. She omitted the part about Mac having been shot in a robbery.

They limped through dinner and rode in silence back to the Learneds' house. Kirsten headed for the front door after a perfunctory goodbye. Bob shrugged and shook his head. Kate said, "Mac needs to get some sleep. If it's okay with you, we'll just park out front for the night."

She led Mac to the RV without waiting for a response.

26

Bad dreams haunted Kate throughout the night. A grinning Jack Nicholson barged into her bedroom and ordered, "Git up! Git yer ass in gear!"

She popped into a sitting position and looked around, struggling to get her bearings.

Mac's arms and legs pumped furiously. It was another seizure. She vaulted from the bed to call for help, but changed her mind as soon as her feet hit the floor. There was no point in dealing with a 911 operator. She could get Mac to the hospital as fast as an ambulance could get to him.

Kate pulled on shorts and a tank top. She checked the GPS and took off. The time was 2:17. She reached the emergency room at 2:25. No traffic at that time of morning. Six hours later, Dr. Mika Weizman walked up to her and said, "You should have called 911."

Kate shrugged. *Ten-minute drive either way. I got him to the ER faster.* "How is he?"

"Stable. We had to remove the tumor to relieve pressure on his brain. The tissue has been sent to the lab for analysis. Can you give me the name of his physician?"

"Barry Jacobs in Annapolis, Maryland." Kate held out a folder she had grabbed on her way out of the RV. "The last doctor who saw him was Sam Yang in Chamberlain, South Dakota."

Weizman ignored the offering. "What medication is he on?"

Kate opened the folder and pointed to a sheet of paper taped to the cover. "This is a summary."

Her gaze wandered, idly taking in her surroundings. She hated big hospitals. This one reminded her of the place where she worked before the incident. Six floors. At least a quarter-mile from one end to the other. Specialty sections branched off at intervals. Patient rooms lined the walls like lockers in a high school.

"How come he's here?" Weizman demanded.

"He came to visit a cousin. She has a home in University Village."

The doctor wagged her head in disgust. "I mean how come he isn't in a hospital getting the medical care he needs?"

"He refused treatment. Dr. Yang has him on chemo. I have him on a diet and exercise regimen."

"That probably explains the condition he's in."

"His condition is explained by the fact that, after a lifetime of doing the right things, he found himself alone and dying from brain cancer. His response was 'Fuck it.'"

Weizman recoiled. Kate continued. "All of that happened before he waltzed into my life."

"And you saw an opportunity to experiment with your fantastical approach to treating cancer."

Kate's fists clenched. *What the fuck are you talking about?* "I decided he needed whatever help I could give him."

"Aren't you the Katherine Graham who worked at St. Elizabeth's in St. Louis?"

She nodded. "I work there."

"You are not in the least qualified to be dealing with something like this."

"I have spent the last ten years working with people living out their last days in a senior care facility. I am more qualified than you."

"You can forget about going back to that job. The report I'm going to file will get you barred from ever working with elderly patients."

"I have a nice job as a restaurant manager lined up."

Weizman shook her head and walked off. Fatigue and despair swept over Kate. A strong desire to be back in St. Louis seized her. There was no good reason to stay in Fairbanks. She might never see Mac again.

She trudged back to the camper, lost in a torrent of ideas, schemes and plans. Maybe getting out of that dreadful building helped. Maybe it was getting off her butt and doing something. Probably the fresh air and sunshine. But it could've been Nicholson screaming at her to "Git yer ass in gear."

The place she called home felt empty and cold. She could not imagine missing anyone as much as she missed the old codger.

Kate called the Geophysical Institute and left a message for Professor Robert Learned. He was the one ally she had in Fairbanks. Then she pushed herself to stay busy while she waited for his call.

The EMTs had used their sheet to move Mac off the bed onto the gurney. Then they pushed the bed out of the way in their rush to get him into the hospital. Kate stowed it properly. Mac's clothes were in a heap on the floor. She picked them up, emptied the pockets, and folded them.

His cell phone was in a shirt pocket. She toyed with it, not wanting to invade his privacy. Curiosity won out. She pressed the power button. The screen lit up. She swiped – app icons popped into view. Mac never bothered with passwords unless he had to.

She found Anne with a Maryland area code in his contact list. The headshot showed a woman with a warm, pleasant smile. She looked like the kind of person you could talk to about anything. Someone who would always boost your spirits. Kate needed to talk to her now. Not possible. But making contact with the love of Mac's life cheered her.

Further down, she spotted Ann Stillwell with a Florida area code. This Ann was a looker. No problem getting attention from men. But she projected a stern, commanding persona -- the offspring of an authoritarian father and a warm, feminine mother. Kate pressed the icon. Her call went straight to voice mail. She identified herself and said, "I need to speak to you about your father." She gave her cell number for the callback.

Mac's son was "Junior" in the contact list. Voice mail again. Kate left the same message.

The scotch called out to her. She hadn't needed a drink this bad in a long time. She couldn't risk running into Weizman or anybody else on the hospital staff with alcohol on her breath.

They had marijuana, but she wasn't in the mood for that. She got down into a lotus position to meditate. That didn't work. She needed to be doing something.

Kate went back to Mac's things. A business card in his wallet caught her attention. "Tereza Ivanova" was written in large red letters across the center. "Therapist" was printed in the bottom left corner. She called the number in the bottom right corner. *What kind of therapy did you submit to, Mac?*

A woman with a husky voice and a thick accent said, "Tereza. How can I help you?"

"My name is Katherine Graham. I am calling about a man who may have been your client."

"What is his name?"

"Donald MacGregor."

"Ah. Yes. How is Donald?"

"Not well. He had a seizure this morning. I brought him to the emergency room. They removed a tumor from his brain. He's recovering in the ICU."

"I see. How can I help?"

"I don't know."

"You called me."

"The doctors won't let me see him. I have to do something to keep from going crazy."

Silence. The pause was so long Kate wondered if the line was dead. "Tereza?"

"Donald will be okay," the husky voice reassured her. "This will all work out. You must be patient."

"I wish I could believe that."

"He calls you Kate. Doesn't he?" The woman was gentle but firm. Kate nodded. Tereza continued, "You are the guardian angel sent to keep him safe. That is no easy task, but your success is guaranteed."

Shit. A nut case. "Thank you for your time."

"Katherine," the voice commanded before she could hang up. "If God is with you, who can stand against you?"

"Well, let's see," Kate retorted. "Hospital security. The medical staff taking care of him. If he dies, …" A thought hit her like a punch in the gut. She had to catch her breath. "When he dies, they will probably charge me with negligent homicide."

"That is not going to happen." Tereza spoke with such confidence it was hard not to believe her. "Help is coming. Doors will open when the time is right. Be patient."

"I hope so," Kate muttered. She was about to hang up. The oracle's voice stopped her. "Katherine."

"What?"

"The child you are carrying is the son of a chieftain. Name him Gregor MacGregor."

The phone fell to the floor as she collapsed into a ball. She lay sobbing, unable to move or even think. Her phone interrupted the crying jag. She sat up and studied the screen. The call was from the Geophysical Institute. "Hello."

"Kate. This is Bob," the voice on the other end said. "What's going on? Are you okay?"

"Mac's in the hospital. They won't let me talk to him."

"Is that why you left so early?"

"I had to rush him to the emergency room. He was having a seizure."

"What can I do?"

"I don't know. I think I need a lawyer."

"Kirsten and I will get over there as soon as we can."

"Thank you."

"You sound terrible. Get some rest. I'll call you as soon as I find out what's going on."

He ended the call. Kate said, "Bye." But the line was already dead. She pulled herself up onto the sofa and stretched out. The pot was in the chest across the aisle. She couldn't summon the energy to get up and roll a joint. Kate folded her hands on her belly. *She has to be wrong. I can't be pregnant. The odds against that have to be a billion to one.*

27

er ringtone startled her from a deep sleep. Kate fumbled for her phone and studied the screen trying to make sense of the caller ID. When she figured out why somebody from the Geophysical Institute would be calling. She answered, "Hello."

"Kate? It's Bob."

The cobwebs began to clear. Kate sat up, swinging her feet to the floor. "Where are you?"

"I'm leaving the university. I'll pick up Kirsten on the way to the hospital."

She gushed, "Great." Too exuberant. She checked the time. Three hours had passed since he had promised to get back as soon as he found out what was going on.

"There's a problem, Kate."

"What's that?" She asked, as if she couldn't guess.

"I've had a couple of conversations with Dr. Weizman. She has agreed to let Mac move in with Kirsten and me. We're arranging for home health care services."

"That makes sense. I can handle that."

"It can't be you," Bob snapped. He switched to conciliatory. "I'm sorry. Weizman is adamant. You are not to be allowed any contact with him."

"What the fuck!"

"I'm sorry," he repeated. "I hope you'll cooperate." He paused for her response. Kate rolled her eyes and listened. Bob continued, "Our priority is to get him out of the hospital, and Dr. Weizman controls that. She will have to approve his discharge."

"She can't keep him in there indefinitely no matter what she may have said or implied."

"How long can she keep him?"

Kate shook her head and conceded, "Good point." But she had been through this before. She knew the realities. The hospital administration would want to move a Medicare patient out as quickly as possible. In all likelihood, they had already assigned Mac's case to a social worker who was preparing to place him in a long-term care facility. Weizman wouldn't be able to hold onto him long.

Bob said, "I suggest you find someplace to park your camper while we work this out."

"How long will that take?"

He sighed. "I don't know. A week. Maybe two."

"You are going to need his insurance information, and you should get a lawyer."

"Yeah. I know. I'll look into lawyers tomorrow."

"I've been thru the process. Why don't you let me help?"

It took an eternity for him to answer, "That's probably a good idea."

"Should I call you in the morning to start making arrangements?"

Bob hedged. "I need some time to think this through. I'll call you."

Kate pocketed her cellphone as she strode to the kitchenette to make coffee and a sandwich. *So, I'm the big problem. Cousin Kirsten will need Mac's insurance information to arrange home services for a blind cripple dying of brain cancer. She's probably guessed it's in the camper. Bet it's never crossed her mind that I'm Mac's legal guardian.*

Possession of the RV was an issue. Kate had it for the time being. It belonged to Mac. He or his legal representative could take possession. If Kirsten won control, she could have Kate evicted. What would she do with it? Mac was never going to drive it again.

Sell it? Then what?

The Learneds had no experience. They had no way of anticipating the nightmare they were rushing into. He was going to need rehab for the next month or two. Living arrangements for Mac were going to be a daunting problem. The couple's home wasn't set up to accommodate an elderly, handicapped man. That could be fixed given enough time and money. But other problems would crop up. It would be unending. Mac's needs would destroy their yuppie lifestyle.

Kate decided to hold off a day before calling Bob to see how things were going. Lawyers moved to the top of her to-do list. She googled "lawyers near fairbanks" and studied the results while finishing a late lunch. Two looked promising. Charles Stevenson, the grandson of Alaska's former governor, agreed to discuss the case with her. His secretary penciled her in for 1:30 but warned that he might have to reschedule. Kate replied, "This case is urgent. A man's life is at stake."

Ball's in my court? Tennis is my game. Here comes my return – right down the line – hard and fast.

She moved to an RV park with weekly rates and picked up a rental car for her legwork.

That left the nagging question: Was she? Or wasn't she? She stopped at a drug store for a pregnancy test kit.

28

A good night's sleep reenergized Kate. She picked out three assisted living facilities and three nursing homes for inspection.

Over the next few hours, she visited two assisted living establishments and one nursing home. At both assisted living facilities, the customer representative advised her that Dr. Learned had contacted them about Mr. MacGregor. She let them know that the professor was just doing preliminary research. He did not have the authority to make decisions for his wife's cousin.

Charles J. Stevenson, Attorney at Law, came out to meet Kate in the reception area. He gave her ninety seconds to justify her claim that a man's life was at stake. After the lawyer heard her pitch, he invited her back to the inner sanctum. She felt at home as soon as she stepped into the room. It looked like Jimmy's office. A computer and stacks of folders sat on a worktable. More stacks of case files lined the walls in neat piles. A young man wearing a white shirt, tie, jeans, and running shoes ambled in as she was getting settled. Charlie said, "Katherine, this is Ted Jones. He'll handle your documents and get your case on the court docket."

They spent the next half-hour reviewing Kate's paperwork. Charlie asked questions while Ted took notes. When she asked why the lawyer wasn't taking notes, Charlie said, "They're too much trouble. If I have a question, I look at Ted's."

Kate dropped in on the third assisted living facility and the remaining two nursing homes before calling it a day.

Mac's phone was blinking for attention when she got back to the RV. Junior had called his dad to find out what was going on. She returned the call. "Donald, this is Katherine Graham."

Pause. "Why are you calling on my dad's phone?"

"It's a long story. I've been traveling with your dad on a cross country trip. He has had a stroke and is in the hospital recovering."

"Dad's in a hospital?" The man shrieked. "Is he alright? Where is he?"

"He had a stroke. He's in the ICU at Fairbanks Memorial."

"Is he okay?"

"Yes. But that's all the doctors will tell me."

"Who the hell are you?"

Kate cringed. "I'm a friend." There was no delicate way to put the rest. "I was with him when he had the seizure, and I brought him to the emergency room."

"Where is he?" He reconsidered. "I mean: Where is the hospital?"

"Fairbanks, Alaska."

"Alaska? What is he doing in Alaska?"

"Visiting a cousin."

Junior objected, "We don't have any family in Alaska."

"You wouldn't necessarily know about her," Kate explained. "Your dad told me he connected with the woman through Ancestry."

"Is this a scam?"

"I doubt it." She cocked her head. "I met her. She seems legit."

"But I don't know anything about you," Junior raged.

"I'm Kate. Do you go by Don, Mac, or Junior?"

"Don."

"Okay, Don, I called you to let you know what was going on. You ignored the number I gave you and called your father. I got your message and called back on his phone. That means I know your father well enough to have access to his phone. I would put him on the line if I could."

"Why can't you put him on the line?"

"He's in the hospital," Kate sighed. "I can't visit him because I'm not family."

After a pause, "What can I do?"

"The cousin and her husband are trying to make arrangements. They want to move your dad to their house when he is discharged."

"In Fairbanks?"

"In Fairbanks."

"I live in Melbourne. He should come down here so Ann and I can take care of him."

"That would be ideal. But I wasn't sure you wanted that."

"Why not, for Christ's sake?"

"He told me that he hadn't seen you in years. He felt abandoned."

"Bullshit," Junior snarled. "Ann and I brought our families up to Annapolis for mom's funeral a couple of months ago. We visited with Dad then."

"That makes sense, but that isn't what he told me."

"Well, that's the truth."

"Okay," Kate soothed. She stood to stretch her legs and drifted to the front of the RV. She looked out the front window collecting her thoughts. "The important thing is figuring out what to do after he leaves the hospital."

"We'll move him down here."

"If that's what he wants."

"What else would he want?"

"I don't know." she looked at the ceiling and shook her head. "I think we need to ask him."

"How do I do that? Call the hospital?"

"That's a good idea, but you may not get through."

"Why not?"

"He may not have a phone in his room. He's probably sedated to control post-operative pain." Kate took a deep breath and exhaled. "They don't know you. They may be reluctant to let you speak to him."

"What if I fly up there and talk to him in person?"

"Not a bad idea, but you should lay some groundwork."

"Such as?"

"Fairbanks Memorial has taken control because they see your father as an elderly man who needs protection. Your dad's cousin is trying to take over. Your claim supersedes those claims, but you will have to establish that you are his son. Once you get him to Melbourne, you will need professional help caring for him."

"Of course."

Kate heard the irritation in the man's voice. She had encountered the attitude before. Even heard things like, "That's just great! Dad never makes it easy. It's always a three-ring circus with him."

She started toward the sofa. According to the clock on the microwave, it was late evening on the east coast. "I've already done some of the legwork. I'm on speaking terms with Kirsten Learned. I've located a couple of lawyers that I think can do the job. I'll text you contact information." She paused. "Of course, you can find a lawyer on your own."

"What's in it for you?"

Kate stretched out on the sofa. "I like your father. We've been traveling together for about a month. I want to see that he's in a good situation."

"Right," he sneered. "The whore with a heart of gold. What are you really after?"

"That was uncalled for," she snarled.

"You want something."

"Look, Don. I called you and your sister. I didn't have to do that." The tension was getting to her. She stood and started back to the cabin. "I could have left you in the dark. Maybe I do want something, but that doesn't change your situation. Call Fairbanks Memorial and confirm that your father is a patient then do whatever you think is best."

"What happens to you if I have him moved to Melbourne?"

"I would like the opportunity to see that he gets there and is properly settled before I drop out of the picture."

"That's it? I won't have to get into some big court battle to settle your claims?"

"You won't have any problems with me. What about your sister?"

"What about her?"

"She hasn't returned my call."

"She was in a car accident two days ago. She's in a coma in Melbourne General."

29

Charlie Stevenson contacted Kate at 8:17 to let her know about an emergency hearing. Mrs. Learned had filed to have herself appointed as the legal guardian. Judge Samantha Connors had agreed to consider both claims at a hearing scheduled for nine because of the urgency of the matter. Kate would have to show up to present her arguments.

The cousin's lawyer argued that Doctor and Mrs. Learned would be best positioned to take care of Mr. MacGregor. They were relatives with a home in Fairbanks, and they had made arrangements for in-home care.

The judge flipped through Kate's paperwork. It was properly signed, witnessed, and notarized. Mac had initialed the paragraph that stated Ms. Graham would become his legal guardian if he should become incapacitated. She looked up and studied Kate. "You understand that I can set this contract aside, if I decide that is what's best for Mr. MacGregor?"

"Yes, Ma'am."

"Explain to me why you waited so long to present these documents and assert your claim as his legal guardian."

"Your Honor, before I respond to that, I wish to notify the court of an important development."

Connors nodded.

Kate said, "I spoke with Mr. MacGregor's son yesterday afternoon. He wants to take over his father's care. He is prepared to fly up here. I believe he is arranging for a lawyer in Fairbanks."

"I was not aware he had children," the judge complained. "The filings don't mention any living relatives other than Mrs. Learned."

"They are mentioned in the will that was part of the package I turned over to my lawyer."

Connors shuffled through the papers, found the will and scanned it. "I see."

"Mr. MacGregor fostered the idea that his children had abandoned him. I took his word for it. After the operation to remove the tumor, I contacted them to let them know what was going on. His son returned my call yesterday."

"What agreements did the two of you reach during your conversation?"

"None. I urged him to get a lawyer in Fairbanks and to investigate senior care options near his home in Melbourne."

"Didn't you have a similar conversation with Mrs. Learned's husband?"

"I offered my services."

"It seems like you want a piece of the action no matter who wins," the judge scoffed.

"I feel responsible for Mr. MacGregor's well-being. Neither his son nor his cousin has any experience with a situation like this."

"Is it fair to assume that you will be out of work once Mr. MacGregor is settled?"

"My position has always been temporary. I have a job and a home waiting for me in St. Louis."

"What are Mr. MacGregor's plans for the future."

"We didn't discuss them."

Judge Connors stared daggers at the woman standing before her. Her voice mocking and incredulous, she said, "You drove across the country with a man you knew to be in poor health and never talked about what he would do when the trip was over?"

Kate held her ground. "The obvious choice would be to get him settled in Florida with his children, but he claimed they didn't want him. He has friends in Annapolis. He could move into a senior living facility there. I told him he could come to St. Louis and live at the senior home where I worked."

"And he never gave any indication of what he planned to do?"

"He changed the subject."

"Why did you agree to this stunt in the first place?"

"He walked into the diner where I was working one night and asked me to sit down with him while he ate. Over dinner, he told me he was driving across the country in an RV. He was obviously in poor health.

That made him a danger to himself and everybody else on the road."

"You just dropped everything and took off with a stranger out of a sense of civic duty?" Her voice oozed sarcasm.

"I liked him. The trip sounded exciting, and I was ready for a vacation."

"Would you give me a number where I can reach the younger Mr. MacGregor?"

Charlie slid a pad in front of Kate. She jotted down the number and gave it to the bailiff. He took it to the judge. She looked it over and nodded. "Was the trip worth it, Ms. Graham?"

"In spades. Did you know there is a ferry that sails up the Alaska coast?"

Connors smiled. "I've taken that cruise."

"Now, I have too."

The judge's smile broadened. "Is there someone here from Fairbanks Memorial?"

A twenty-something brunette stood. "Dr. Marie Sutherland, Your Honor."

"Can I arrange an interview with the patient?"

"Yes. He's conscious and coherent."

Connors' face registered surprise. "That was fast."

"I would say his recovery borders on the miraculous."

The judge grinned. "We will take a fifteen-minute recess."

Sutherland sauntered over and extended her hand. "Kate, I'm Marie."

"Kate?"

"You are Nurse Graham, Ms. Graham, or Kate, depending on his mood."

Kate took the proffered hand. "How is he really doing?"

"Quite well. He's cantankerous and demanding. I'm sure he'll be able to go home by the end of the week."

"Good. Now we just have to figure out where 'home' is." She was glad to hear Mac was on the mend but hurt that she couldn't visit.

"Dr. Weizman wants you to come by her office."

Kate's lips curled into a sardonic smile. "So I can review her report?"

Marie kept her cool. "She's changed her mind."

Kate's brows arched. The intern continued. "Dr. Yang asked about you. He told us how impressed he was with the way you handled things." She smirked. Her eyes twinkled. "And Mr. MacGregor has made a remarkable recovery. That means you did a good job of maintaining his health before the seizure."

"When?"

"She asked that you drop by after the hearing."

Judge Connors returned to the bench and announced, "This hearing will be continued in three days. At that time, Mr. Donald MacGregor Jr will present his case for being the legal guardian. In the meantime, the court will appoint a social worker to evaluate the elder Mr. MacGregor. The court appoints Ms. Graham to be his legal guardian until further notice. Fairbanks Memorial is hereby ordered to grant her unrestricted access to her client."

Kate walked out of the courthouse feeling a thousand pounds lighter. She was famished. An Italian sub was not at the top of the nutritional food chain. But that's what she felt like. That's what she got. And a lemon-lime soda, pretending that was a healthy choice because of the vitamin C. For the first time in days, she relaxed and enjoyed a meal.

Mac smiled when she walked into his room. Her eyes teared up. It was all she could do to keep from crawling into bed with him. *Kissing him like a lost puppy.*

"Whe' can I ge' outta here?"

Kate stepped to his bedside and pulled his hand to her lips for a kiss. "Give it a couple of more days," she said, "that was a serious operation."

He glowered. "I ain' gaw time ta be inna hosp't'l."

"Why?" She eyed him suspiciously. "You got plans? You got somethin' goin' on I don't know about?"

"Nah," Mac laughed. "Hunner thin's I rather be doin'."

"Such as?"

"We coul' drive down da coas'," he suggested. "Always wanna drive Highway One."

"What about Melbourne?" She countered.

He glared and growled, "Ain' gonna hap'n."

"We have to talk about what is going to happen."

"Why? Wuz wron'?"

Kate looked up at the ceiling to hide her tears. "You need to find a place to settle down. Traveling around in that RV is too hard on you."

"Me?" He shot her a look. "Or you?"

"Both."

"Qui' if you wan'."

"Where would that leave you?"

"I figger ou' sumpen."

"I will never quit on you. We've been through that. But it's not like before. You can't drive. You can't even take care of yourself. You need help – a lot of help."

He looked away. His breath came in short angry puffs. When he turned back, he grumbled, "We wouldn' have dis probl'm if you le' me die like I was s'pposed ta."

She bit her lip and fought back tears. "I couldn't do that."

He stared at her. When she could no longer stand it, Kate said, "I'll stay with you as long as you want me, but you need to decide where you want to settle down."

"Guess I don' have a choice."

"There was a hearing this morning. I'm in charge for now, so you have some choices. When the hearing reconvenes, Don Junior will be there with a lawyer. The court will probably put him in charge of making those decisions."

"Why's he involve'?"

"I called him."

Mac let go of her hand. "Ge' ou'," he roared.

"He's your son. I had to tell him sooner or later."

"Hasn' been ma son for years. Now he's ma boss?"

"He came to Anne's funeral."

"He 'n' his sisser show' up da nigh' 'fore da fun'r'l. Jus' in time ta pay respec'. Den dey get hotel rooms.

Dey attend da fun'r'l 'n' da burial. Dey hang ou' wi' der frenns. Dey leave wit'ou' sayin' goo'-bye."

"Oh."

"Get ou'," he barked.

Kate shook her head. There was nothing to say. She turned and left the room.

30

Kate found a seat in the lobby outside Mac's room. She slumped. The more she thought about things, the more certain she became that it was over. Mac was stubborn. He wouldn't bend. Don Junior would show up in court with his lawyer. Connors would have no choice but to make him the legal guardian and he would take his father to Melbourne. She was officially a fifth wheel.

People with a reason for being in that hospital paraded past her outpost. Visit a loved one. Deliver meds. Bring a meal. Collect blood. She no longer had a purpose. A reason to be there. Sure, she'd been sleeping with him. And maybe she had an ace to play. But those were not legal grounds for making her the guardian. Those things would just make her look bad.

Kate tried to find a book that would cheer her up and get her over the hump. They don't write books about heroines who sit in a hospital lobby waiting for something to happen. She called Sam Reinhart.

"Sam, I'm sorry to bother you but I need to talk to somebody."

"What is it, bubelah?"

"Mac got mad, and kicked me out of his room."

"His room?"

"He had a stroke. He's in the hospital recovering."

"And what was the unforgivable sin?"

"I called his children to let them know he was in the hospital."

They talked for an hour while Sam caught up on Kate's adventures and pieced together the current situation. He managed to lighten her mood in the process. "You shouldn't be with an old man. They're such kvetches. My back hurts. Why does your back hurt? It's Monday. My knees ache. Why? It's Wednesday."

She had to smile. "You're an old man. You know."

"Do I sleep in your bed?" That got a chuckle. He said, "It is too soon to quit. Waiting isn't glamorous but sometimes ..."

"How long am I supposed to just sit here?"

"Until it is time to do something."

"That's no help," Kate quipped.

"You are a smart woman. You will figure it out."

"If I believed that I wouldn't be talking to you."

"Then we are both lucky your faith is weak." Sam paused as if letting that sink in. "Bubelah, if I told you there will be a sign, you would demand. 'What sign?' I don't know that. Don't ask me. Just wait for it."

"Okay, Sam. Thanks. And I love you."

When visiting hours ended, Kate dragged herself back to the camper. She returned to her post first thing in the morning. It felt like she hadn't slept. Her tablet had gone through the entire book she had curled up with. She could only remember the first chapter. Sleep had clearly gotten the best of her.

The court-appointed social worker showed up around ten. Dr. Sutherland escorted the woman to Mac's room. Kate was too far away to hear any of the conversation but it must have been frustrating. The social worker went straight to Kate and said, "He certainly is stubborn."

"Did you get what you needed?"

The woman extended her hand. "Jeanne Wilson."

"Katherine Graham."

"I think I got enough, but I have some questions for you." Kate nodded. Wilson asked, "How long have you known Mr. MacGregor?"

"Six weeks."

"Would you say you know him well?"

"Yes."

"You mentioned some options to Judge Connors, but you didn't say anything about him staying with his cousin here in Fairbanks."

"Kirsten and her husband made a generous offer. I don't believe they should be taking care of Mr. MacGregor over the long haul."

"What about his son?"

"He's committed. I think it's a bigger job than he imagines, but we are talking about his father. Besides, he has a sister to share the burden."

"Has anyone spoken with the sister?"

"According to Don Junior, she's in Melbourne General recovering from a car accident."

"You also mentioned St. Louis."

"I'm not a relative, but I care for the elderly. I've checked with St. Elizabeth's Senior Living Facility and I could get him in."

"That's where you work?"

"Yes."

Wilson made some notes. She looked up. "Thank you."

Kate jumped in. "Dr. Sutherland."

"Yes?"

"When will Mr. MacGregor be able to leave the hospital?"

"He could leave now if he had someplace to go."

"We'll decide where to put him at the hearing," Wilson said.

Kate let them get out of sight before going back into Mac's room. The head of his bed had been raised halfway. A pile of pillows supported him in a sitting position while he watched TV. He didn't acknowledge her. She lowered the railing on the side of his bed and pushed the tubes out of her way as she sidled next to him. He let her take his hand, but he didn't squeeze back. "Mac, please listen to me." He kept his focus on the TV. Her fingers ran across the bandage on his head. She guessed it bothered her more than him. It was a done deal. Tangible evidence of her failure to take care of him. They had operated on him. It was her fault. "Do you remember how we — you and

I together — were able to get Dr. Yang to go along with our approach?"

His eyes flitted in her direction. "When I brought you in here, you were almost dead. Your doctor blamed me. She said I couldn't have any more contact with you." Now his head turned. His eyes locked on hers. "That destroyed me. I didn't know what to do. I went back to the RV and started cleaning up the mess. Your phone fell out of your pocket. It took a while but I looked through your contacts. I found Anne. She looks so beautiful, warm and friendly. You were lucky to have her for a companion. Then I found your daughter and I felt sure she would want to know about her father's situation. So, I called her and left a message. And Junior. I called and left a message because I thought he had a right to know."

Kate pulled Mac's fingers to her lips and kissed them. "I was desperate. I needed help. Somebody. Anybody. I called Bob." Mac was now fully engaged. "He called me back later and said he and Kirsten were planning to take care of you after you were discharged."

"Dey volunteer'?"

"Yes, and they started looking into home health care services so you would get the care you need."

He pressed his lips into a grim line and shook his head. Kate continued, "Bob told me your doctor insisted that I could not be involved." Mac shifted around to face her directly. "I was in a dark place." He squeezed her hand. "Then I spotted a business card in your stuff." His brows arched. "I called Tereza."

Mac looked mystified. Then a light went on. He nodded. "Her. Wha' she say?"

"Help would come, and doors would open."

He nodded again. "Sounns like 'er."

"Junior called back the next day. I told him everything. He said you should come to Melbourne so he and Ann could take care of you."

"He say da'?"

"Yes."

"On his own?"

"Yes. He offered to fly up here and make arrangements."

"Wha' abou' Ann?"

"She was in a car accident a few days ago. She's still in a coma as far as I know."

Mac looked like he wanted to say something but couldn't get the words out. Kate held out his phone. "Call Junior and ask him."

She walked to the window while they talked. Mac seemed to be warming to the idea of moving to Melbourne. After he hung up, he said, "Kate." His voice was husky.

She turned back to face him. "Wha' are you gonna do?"

"Are you asking about *us*?"

He closed his eyes and stroked his chin. He nodded. "Yeah." He still sounded choked. "Wha' happens ta *us*?"

"I can move to Melbourne if that's what you want."

"Probly bes'. Ann's conscious. Serious condition bu' shoul' recover. I gotta see her."

"If that's what you want, we can get started today. I'll tell Junior he doesn't have to come up here. We'll go down there. You can sign yourself out, and we'll hit the road."

"In da camper?"

"Sure. Why not?"

"Long drive."

"I'll put *you* on a plane if you want. I'm not leaving without that RV."

He shook his head in disbelief. "Why?"

"It's our home. That's where I plan to live the rest of my life."

Mac rolled his eyes up to the ceiling. When he turned back to Kate, he said, "Probly easier 'n flyin'."

He waved her over. Squeezed her to his chest and pressed her cheek against his. She kissed him on the neck as she pushed away. "I have a lot to do and not much time. Please don't say anything until I get back. This has to be our secret."

Mac smiled and nodded. Kate called Charlie Stevenson with an urgent request for immediate help. He was with a client, but he took the call. "What do you need?"

"Mac has agreed to move to Melbourne. I want to get him out of the hospital as soon as possible."

"Is he well enough to leave?"

"Dr. Sutherland told me he was."

"The hearing is still two days away."

"We don't need the hearing. Mac has expressed his desire to move to Melbourne with his son."

"Why the sudden change?"

"His daughter is in critical condition. He's anxious to see her."

"What do you want from me?"

"Mac is going to have to check himself out. We could use your support."

"Okay. I can meet you at the hospital in about twenty minutes."

"I have to drop off my rental and pick up our RV."

"I'll meet you at the rental office."

Things were finally going her way. She needed one more favor from Charlie – a little help getting Mac on board the camper. The old man wouldn't be able to do much in his condition. Kate had bought him a pair of walking forearm crutches, but there was no time to train him.

Dr. Weizman was in surgery. Sutherland managed the checkout. She talked to Don Junior to make sure he had made arrangements on his end. Then she called Melbourne General to confirm that Ann was a patient. She wrote prescriptions for meds and pain killers. Then she walked them through the pharmacy.

Charlie drove Kate and Mac back to the RV. He helped get the old man settled and waited while Kate dealt with the rental manager. They hugged as she was about to step into the camper. The lawyer said, "You aren't going to put him on a plane. Are you?"

"Nope."

He shook his head. "Good Luck. It's a long drive. Crossing Canada is going to be a challenge."

"At least traffic won't be a problem."

Kate hugged him again and gave him a sisterly peck on the cheek. He left for his office.

31

Kate closed the camper's door and went straight to the captain's chair. She watched Charlie Stevenson's car pull away. *Okay. This is it. Gotta get organized.*

A check of the GPS told her it was 5000 miles to Melbourne, Florida. Mac would need his meds every six hours. Coincidentally the RV would need gas about every six hours. Gas stations might not be readily available, but she could find them using Google. She decided her best strategy would be taking care of Mac when she stopped for gas.

A closer look at the route showed that the Canadian border was about six hours away and there was an RV Park a half-hour beyond the crossing. Route 2 would take them from Fairbanks to the campground. She made a reservation and gave Mac his meds.

They set out for Melbourne around 4. The highway followed the Tanana River as it snaked between mountains on the left and a valley on the right. It took them through North Pole, Moose Creek, and the Eielson Air Force Base. They stopped at Delta

Junction for gas and a bite to eat. Kate found a mirror to put in the kitchenette so she and Mac could keep an eye on each other.

Mac dozed off as soon as they started driving again. Kate pulled up *The Last Widow* by Karin Slaughter. She had become a fan of the Will Trent series years earlier. She moved on. Slaughter kept writing. That gave Kate several books to keep her company.

Outside Delta Junction, the highway turned away from the river and headed straight across the Yukon toward the border crossing. It took them through a mountain pass as it wound around the southwest border of the Tanana State Forest. They breezed through the Canadian border checkpoint a little after nine. Kate checked into Beaver Creek RV Park around ten. Just in time for Mac's meds.

They had only traveled 300 miles, but they had taken the proverbial first step.

Kate wanted to get out and walk around but wrestling Mac down the stairs and back up was out of the question. She walked back to the bed where he was resting. "You've been lying around for four days. You need to get up and exercise."

"T'm'rrow."

"Let's do a little now. Tomorrow you can do more."

Mac balked. He scrunched up his nose and shook his head. Kate said, "You have exercised every day of this trip. Well almost every day. It's even more important now and fitting it in is going to be a challenge. We have to take advantage of every opportunity."

Mac didn't move a muscle. Kate took his hands and pulled him into a sitting position. "There," she said. "That's not so bad. Is it?"

Mac shrugged. Kate looped her right arm behind his knees and scooped his legs over the edge of the bed. She went to the closet and retrieved crutches she had bought. "Whuz da'?" Mac asked.

"Crutches. You're going to need them from now on."

"Can' use 'em."

"That'll have to change."

"Why?"

"You don't want to fall and crack your head. And I don't want to throw my back out helping you up." Kate stroked his head and kissed him. "Come on, Mac. This is important." She pulled on his right elbow. He slid to the floor. She helped him get his arms in the sleeves on the crutches. "Just walk to the shower and back."

By the time Mac reached the shower, he had established a little rhythm. He seemed comfortable walking back. Kate made him walk all the way to the microwave. She smiled and kissed him. "Can you do it again?"

He grimaced, but he turned and made his way to the shower, then back to the microwave. Kate greeted him with a broad smile. "How about you do eight more."

"Yer messin' w' me," Mac complained.

"Ten is a nice round number."

"So'z two."

"Do eight more and you can get back to your book while I stretch my legs."

Mac would have objected but he wasn't going to win. He marched to the shower and back eight more times. Kate helped him get settled on the bed, gave him a kiss, and went out for a walk.

The sun was still high in the sky when she got back to the camper. Mac was sound asleep. She rolled her sleeping bag out on the floor so he could have the bed to himself. She pulled on a sleeping mask to block out the light and talked herself into relaxing for a few hours' sleep.

When her alarm summoned her back to consciousness, she gave Mac his meds, made coffee, and tidied up. Her plan was ambitious. 800 miles in three shifts. Starting with a 300-mile jaunt to the territorial capital, Whitehorse. They were on the road by 5. The highway carried them south through rolling hills. Kluane National Park and the St. Elias Mountains were on their right. Mount Logan, the second-highest mountain in North America, towered in the distance.

A couple of hours later, Kate paused at the Talbot Arms motel, the only business in the town of Destruction Bay. It was the perfect place to stop for a cup of coffee and a fill-up. She was not going to risk running out of gas.

It took a couple of more hours to reach Haines Junction, an actual town where the road from Haines on the coast connects with the Alcan Highway. She needed to stretch her legs, grab a carry-out brunch and fill the tank.

Mac announced he was going to stretch his legs as well. He was sitting on the edge of the bed. "You mean like last night?" Kate asked.

"I nee' fresh air."

"You'll have to put on some clothes," Kate sighed. "And we'll have to figure out how to negotiate steps."

"I can hannle steps."

Kate helped him dress. Another new indignity for Mac. He made his way to the exit and paused. Supporting himself against the walls, he worked his way down the steps. She followed. He froze when he reached the bottom step. It was a long way to the ground. She handed him the crutches. "Use these for support."

Mac turned to her with a blank, uncomprehending stare. The words made no sense. She put one of his arms into the sleeve on a crutch and then the other arm. Turning him back to the exit, she helped him lower the crutches to the ground. It was awkward. He was unsteady. But he made it safely to the surface of the parking lot. From there he was able to walk to the front of the store.

Inside, they saw barstools at a food counter but no seats Mac could use. Kate ordered steak and eggs to go. They browsed while they waited. No one seemed to pay much attention to an old man with a bandage around his head. Probably too polite.

When they got back to the camper, Kate had to take their meal up and come back down to help Mac. Once he got past the first step, he was able to get to the top without much trouble. They ate and Kate got

Mac settled. She filled the tank and took off for the next stop.

The stopover had been a success. Mac had gotten out of the camper and back in. And he had used his crutches.

Highway 1 left Haines Junction heading east across the mountainous terrain that characterizes the south end of the Yukon. Whitehorse, the capital of the Yukon Territory, is a modern city with reminders of the gold rush days. It sat at the edge of the Yukon River with mountains rising up behind it. Kate and Mac passed through without stopping. They continued to a rest stop on the shores of the McClintock River an hour further on.

It was time for Mac's meds and Kate's power nap. She put him through 20 minutes of physical therapy before curling up next to him. An hour later, she popped up and returned to her seat in the cockpit. She was looking at a seven-hour push to the RV Park near Muncho Lake, where she intended to spend the night.

Kate gassed up at Johnson's crossing. She stopped again at the Nugget City Gas Station and Restaurant. They ventured out for dinner. Mac joked, "Anudder Ee Vee Ay."

"EVA?"

"Exra Ve'ic'lar Act'v'ty."

Kate grinned. "Yeah."

Fifteen minutes after they left the restaurant, Highway 1 came to an end. They found themselves heading southeast across British Columbia on Route

97. Kate checked into the Muncho Lake RV Park around 10. She gave Mac his meds and another physical therapy session before sinking into a deep sleep.

Mac got his meds again at 4. Kate made a couple of omelets in the microwave and served them with coffee. She gassed up the RV and shoved off. The highway wound through the northern Rockies. They took advantage of a rest stop a couple of hours later. Another chance for Mac to practice his EVA skills. They began their descent from the high mountains an hour after that. They stopped for gas at Fort Nelson, a modest community in the foothills on the eastern edge of the Rockies, before continuing south to Pink Mountain. They stopped at the Buffalo Inn for Mac's meds and a quick meal, then on to Fort St. John where Kate found a spot overlooking a lake for her big break. Physical therapy for him and a power nap for her.

The next target was Edmonton, 400 miles away. Kate made reservations at an RV park north of the city. She gassed up and took off. They paused again to gas up at one of those modern truck stops with a decent food court. The couple went inside for dinner after Mac got his meds. They made it to the RV park a little after 8.

Edmonton, with a million people, a hockey team and a football team, anchors the northwestern corner the Great Plains. They had reached civilization. Another day's drive would put them back in the US.

Kate was up at 4 and had them on the road an hour later. They rolled through Edmonton's north end on Highway 15. Then on to North Battleford, where they stopped for gas and brunch.

They stopped again in Chamberlain for a short break. Mac got his meds and Kate filled the tank. They came across a historic marker while stretching their legs. It informed them that this tiny rural community was part of a trail named in honor of nineteenth-century politician and renegade Louis Riel. The son of a Native American and a French settler, he led Native Americans along Canada's Red River in dealings with the Canadian Government. He was tried and executed for his part in a raid that resulted in the deaths of some French-Canadian settlers.

They took their long break just across the border at Portal, North Dakota. Two hours later, they drove into Minot, Kate's final destination for the day.

She had gotten them from Fairbanks, Alaska, across Canada to Minot, North Dakota, in three days. They could make it to Melbourne in another four if she kept up that pace.

They had some time to take in the sights such as they were. An Air Force base was the main attraction. They dined in a restaurant. Mac wanted apple pie and coffee for dessert. He took a bite or two, put his fork down and stared at her. "Le'z stop in Sain' Loous."

She shrugged. "Okay."

"Leg'l wor' fer yer cuz'n."

"What kind of legal work if you don't mind my asking."

"Change my will."

"I don't think you should put me in your will. All I want is the camper."

He grimaced. His expression scared her. Kate was certain that whatever was about to come out was terrible. When he finally spoke, he said, "Will you marry me?"

She burst out laughing. He recoiled. She clamped a hand on her mouth. "I'm sorry." She shook her head. "I didn't mean that." She was giddy. Beaming from ear to ear. "I would be happy to marry you. But I like us the way we are."

She heard the words as if someone at another table had spoken them.

He nodded. "Fer now. Bu' we're movin' in wi' Anne's kids. Yer an ou'sid'r." He shook his head. "Can' have dat." He took a breath and puffed out through his nose. "We're one flesh. I wan' da worl' ta know."

Her defenses crumbled. No one had ever said anything like that to her. She almost blurted out her secret. Instead, she bowed her head and closed her eyes. She felt tears welling up and running down her cheeks. Looking back up at him, she wiped the tears away and said in a choked voice, "Yes, Donald Mac-Gregor. I will marry you."

32

Mac was exhausted by the time they got back to the RV. He dropped off to sleep almost immediately. Kate, on the other hand, was pumped. She sat on the edge of the bed for a few minutes before deciding she was too restless to cuddle with Mac. She rolled out her sleeping bag and lay down but couldn't concentrate long enough to get through the mechanics of self-hypnosis. The scene in the restaurant would not let her go. Mac's proposal had come out of nowhere. Very romantic and very bizarre. Her acceptance was absolutely insane. No regrets. She had no intention of walking away from the old man. But it was like an earthquake ripping her world apart.

She took scotch in a cup to the cockpit, where she sat in the captain's chair and brooded. Kate was still sitting there when the chirping alarm woke her. The cup rested against her crotch in a vee formed by her thighs. It still held a swig of the magic liquid. She emptied it in the sink, gave Mac his meds, and made a quick breakfast. Then off for St. Louis. She had to stop and give Mac his meds when they reached Rochester, Minnesota.

Her GPS was estimating nine more hours to her hometown, assuming moderate traffic. The drive to Camp Discovery could take 12 hours if the traffic was heavier than expected. Eddie was an impeccable host but Kate didn't want to impose on him at that time of night.

Her mood was the real problem. She didn't feel like spending another day on the road. Convincing Mac to lay over in Rochester wasn't hard. He was ready for a break. Kate found a place to park the camper for the rest of their stay and hired an Uber driver to take them into town.

As a bonus, the woman gave them a tour. She drove them past the IBM Complex. At one time, it had housed the company's largest operations.

She took them to see the headquarters of the Mayo Clinic. A century ago, the Mayo Clinic was a clinic. In 2019, it was the world's largest hospital.

The Mayo Building was a massive multi-story structure. The Mayo Clinic Hospital, across the street, was another enormous edifice. These buildings were surrounded by a network of smaller buildings that comprised the downtown campus. There was a satellite campus a few blocks north and another satellite campus a few blocks south. As the couple sat in the back of a late model Camry Hybrid listening to the driver's spiel, Kate whispered, "Maybe you should go in and get them to take a look at you."

"I ain' da' sick."

She nuzzled him and teased, "You're dying, sweetheart."

"Yeah? Wha' dey gon' do abou' dat?"

Stunned, Kate wrapped her arms around him and squeezed with all her strength. She sobbed softly against his chest.

The driver interrupted. "Where to now?"

Kate looked up, a hint of tears in her eyes. "We'd like to ride the trolley."

The trolley tours were a great way to see a city like Rochester. "Hop-on Hop-off." Riders could get off one trolley to check out an attraction and hop back on a later trolley to continue the tour. That worked well for most tourists. Mac was in no condition to take advantage of the opportunity.

They did get off when Kate spotted a stand renting out bikes. She was able to get a tandem trike with the stoker's seat in the front, which was the reverse of the standard configuration for tandems. The arrangement gave Mac an unobstructed view, but Kate had to do all the pedaling. She managed.

Miles of bike trails carried them through parks and along lakes. When they came to Soldier Field, Rochester's memorial to the country's war dead, Kate stopped so they could pay their respects. But Mac got antsy after a few minutes. "Lez go."

Kate nodded. "Okay."

"Know why dey honor da dead?" He asked as she helped him into his seat.

"Sacrificing your life for your country is a big deal."

"Iz easier 'n tinkin' abou' da wounded."

Kate shut her eyes, looked down, and shook her head. She was biting on her lower lip when she looked back up. "Let's take this thing back and get some dinner."

She returned the rented trike and got a ride back to the camper so Mac could get his meds and a nap. A few hours later, they returned to the city for dinner at one of the pubs that offered locally brewed ale and fresh food from nearby farms.

Then back into the routine. Physical therapy and meds for Mac.

They were up again at 4 and on the road by 5. Kate had to push hard to get her fiancée to her cousin's office a little after noon. She parked in front of the building ahead of schedule. Mac showered and put on a clean outfit.

His meeting with the lawyer lasted thirty minutes.

Kate drove him to St. Elizabeths to be evaluated. Dr. Gert Williams set up a teleconference with Dr. Marie Sutherland in Fairbanks. The two women chatted while Williams examined Mac and replaced his bandage. The wound from the operation was healing as expected. Dr. Weizman popped in to watch. She had to register her disapproval of the way Kate had gone about things.

"Katherine is a valued member of our team. She's diligent, and she knows her stuff," Williams countered.

"Her behavior has been unethical at best."

"Mr. MacGregor's recovery seems to be on schedule. It looks like Katherine is doing everything that can be done."

"She pulled Mr. MacGregor out of the hospital and left Fairbanks while a judge was trying to determine who should be responsible for his care."

"It is my understanding that Mr. MacGregor's son plans to take on those duties." Williams paused as if waiting for a rebuttal. "Isn't that correct, Dr. Sutherland?"

The intern blushed and cleared her throat. "Yes. That's correct. I confirmed it in a phone conversation with Mr. MacGregor."

Weizman glared at her assistant. Williams said, "The son's claim supersedes all other claims."

"She should have let Judge Connors make that call," Weizman snapped.

"Katherine is Mr. MacGregor's legal guardian. She did what she thought was best under the circumstances."

"What circumstances are those?"

Gert looked over at Kate. Smiled and winked. "She loves Mr. MacGregor." Kate felt her cheeks turning red.

"Then, she should stop passing herself off as his caregiver."

"And Mr. MacGregor was ready to go to Florida to be with his children. It has been nice talking with you, Dr. Weizman," Williams said. "I have to get going. I'm behind schedule." With that, she killed the link.

They drove to Sam's Diner when they left the clinic. Kate ordered spaghetti and meatballs and a Cabernet. She called Eddie to let him know they were planning on staying at Camp Discovery. Sam appeared with their wine and asked if he could join them. "How long will you be in town?"

"It looks like two or three days," Kate said. "Might be a week. Jimmy is making arrangements for the wedding. The JP is booked solid at the moment."

"Who is getting married?"

"We are," Mac growled.

Sam smiled and nodded. "You should have your reception here."

"That's a nice offer," Kate said. "I'd like that."

"We could do it tomorrow night."

"If we were marrie'," Mac grumbled.

"Tomorrow. Just before the reception," Sam proposed.

"JP won' do i' t'morrow," Mac countered. "Awready check'."

"My rabbi will."

"We're naw Jews," Mac objected.

Sam countered, "No one is going to hold that against you."

Kate said, "I think Mac meant a Jewish ceremony wouldn't be appropriate."

Sam grinned. "So, you want a nobody to stand there and listen while you promise to love each other?"

She clamped her lips shut and shook her head. Sam frowned at Mac, then turned to Kate with a twinkle in his eyes. "Rabbi Zenman is very smart. He can be a justice of the peace when he wants."

She reached under the table and squeezed Mac's hand. "We would be pleased to have him officiate if he's willing."

"Then it's settled. You two relax and enjoy your dinner. I will make the arrangements and let you know when to show up."

Sam's proposal was a godsend. Kate knew people were unhappy about her decision to drive. She knew Junior well enough to guess how he was feeling. Getting stuck in St. Louis for a week would have been the last straw. No matter that Mac had requested the stop to meet with his lawyer.

Kate was enjoying the visits with her friends much more than she had expected. But tomorrow, she would have to impose on those friends to drop everything so they could attend her spur-of-the-moment wedding.

Eddie stopped by to see how they were doing. He brought dinner. Kate thanked him. But they couldn't do it justice after the meal they had just eaten. Could they put it in the fridge for tomorrow? Maybe he would like to come in for a beer. He held out the skillet he was using as a tray. Their hands touched. A thrill shot through her. She didn't dare look him in the eye.

Kate squeezed the skillet into their small refrigerator. Eddie busied himself with rearranging the couch into two bench seats facing each other across the table. He took the seat next to Mac. That left the seat facing them for Kate. She couldn't avoid looking at that beautiful brown face and the sparkling eyes that carried on a silent conversation with her. She did her best to ignore the warm glow in her chest.

Mac struggled to talk about their trip. Eddie used his own experiences to help the conversation along.

He had traveled the Lewis and Clark Trail and spent time in Denali National Park. One Wounded Warrior outing had included a climb on the mountain itself. Kate had to provide details about their trip across the Yukon. Eddie kept her talking. He was familiar with the terrain from a training mission his unit had completed years earlier.

Kate's phone rang. It was Jimmy calling with details about the wedding. She interrupted his data dump to bring Eddie up to speed and invite him to the festivities. He accepted. Jimmy promised to pass the information to Sam. Then he suggested that he and his secretary, Mrs. Burns, could be the witnesses. He also offered to be the best man with Mrs. Burns as maid of honor. Kate glanced over at Mac and Eddie sitting together. In a flash, she knew who Mac's best man should be. She told Jimmy she would get back to him after she had discussed it with the groom.

Before he hung up, Jimmy offered to drive Kate and Mac around for sightseeing and shopping before the wedding. Kate suggested 10 in the morning.

After Eddie left, Kate went over the phone conversation with Mac. He said, "Too much. Why we 'ave ta go shoppin'?"

"Well," Kate said, trying to be reasonable. "We need rings. I would like to wear something dressy."

"I wanna simple. Civ'l cer'mony. JP. Ge' i' ov'r wi',"

"This is my wedding too," Kate shot back. "And these are my friends. I want to share my big moment with them."

Mac pressed his lips together and snorted. He wasn't ready to deal with the situation.

Kate brought up the issue again after breakfast in the morning. "Why don't you ask Eddie to be your best man?"

"Ain' import'n'. Don' nee' one."

"It might be important to him," Kate objected. Mac looked puzzled. "He obviously cares about us. He came over for a visit last night."

"I dunno. Too much hassle."

"It won't be the end of the world if he turns you down," Kate said. Mac rejected the idea with a sneer and a shake of his head. Kate purred, "But if he says yes, you'll have one of your favorite people standing by your side when you marry me."

"Too early ta call."

"We've got time."

"You gonna ge' a maida honor?"

"Gert Williams. If you get Eddie."

"Wha' if she sez no?"

"She won't."

The place was packed when Mac and Kate walked in. Eddie and Gert were waiting at the door. They ushered the couple to the middle of the room. Mac was wearing tan slacks and a black shirt. He wore a fedora to hide the bandage. She wore pink slacks with a matching blazer over a black blouse.

Rabbi Zenman rose and walked over to greet them. He did a good job covering the shock that came with meeting Mac for the first time. He soldiered on, reading the standard marriage vows with the traditional, "Do you take this person to be your spouse?"

Then he paused to study them thoughtfully. "I have a blessing for the couple, but I'm not sure it's appropriate in this case."

"I think you should use it," Kate said. "It might be more appropriate than you imagine."

He bit his lip and tilted his head slightly. Then he intoned:

"Blessed are you, O Lord our God, King of the universe, who has created joy and gladness, bridegroom and bride, mirth and exultation, pleasure and delight, love and brotherhood, peace and friendship.

"O Lord, make these beloved companions greatly rejoice even as you rejoiced at your creation in the Garden of Eden. Blessed are you, O Lord, who makes the bridegroom and bride to rejoice.

"Mr. and Mrs. MacGregor, may you be inspired each day by the world around you. May the people you meet show you love and friendship, generosity, kindness, and compassion. May you express these qualities freely throughout your lives.

"You may kiss the bride."

Mac pulled Kate in for a kiss. He still had it. She stared at him, unable to believe how happy and proud she felt. This was the moment.

"I have something for you, Mr. MacGregor," Kate said. The room went quiet. She giggled nervously. Her heart pounded against her chest. Her palms felt moist. With no idea how he would react, she blurted out, "A son."

Mac looked lost. If he had heard what she said, he wasn't making sense of it. "I'm pregnant," Kate barked anxiously. "Tereza said it would be a boy, and we should name him Gregor MacGregor."

"Gregory," Mac said at last. "Gregory Donal' Ma'Gregor. We're nah given da boy a weir' name."

Applause broke out. She threw her arms around Mac's neck and whispered in his ear, "I love you."

33

Kate was happy. And terrified. When they got back to the camper, she did her best. Mac got his meds but physical therapy was out of the question. They were too exhausted. They cuddled and slept. Kate's body relaxed. Her frazzled brain let go and shut down. She climbed back to REM level. An ominous dream took over her mind and body.

She was back in Sam's diner. She and Mac had said their "I dos." Bing Crosby played the piano and sang:

It's beginning to look a lot like Christmas.

It's snowing silver dollars,

And money's growing on trees.

The bells of St. Mary's

Are ringing for your wedding.

Aren't you glad you're you?

Mac escorted her out of the diner to a sidewalk on a street lined with manicured lawns and one-story ranches. They approached one in the middle of the block. Mac was smiling. He seemed happier than he'd ever been. She only realized he wasn't using his crutches when he held the door. She stepped past him into the crowded living room. Don Junior and Ann and their spouses and kids were assembled on the other side of the room facing her. She said, "Hi. I'm your new mom."

They charged like rabid zombies. Kate raced out the door and down a winding path through a forest. She tripped and reached out to break her fall. When she felt herself hit the ground, a myoclonic jerk snapped her back to reality.

Sitting up, she surveyed the dark, eerily quiet interior of the camper. Mac was sound asleep, one hand resting on her thigh. She pulled it to her lips. He didn't stir. She laid it across his chest. It slid off and dropped to the mattress. Kate wriggled past him to get to the floor. She paused to study him. He was sleeping the sleep of the medicated. Nothing was going to wake him.

She poured a little scotch and made her way to the cockpit. She sat and took a swig. Then she remembered little Gregory Donald MacGregor, or should it be Donald Gregory MacGregor. That had a better rhythm. At any rate, no more scotch for the time being.

Kate quickly came up with the Bing Crosby connection. Kathryn Grandstaff, the crooner's second wife, was about the same age as his children when they married. Most of the sensation had subsided by the time Kate read about Kathy Crosby. She fixated on the woman because they were both Kathy's. The glamour fascinated her. Now she saw the story in a different light.

Sitting in the darkened cockpit, staring at a sky filled with stars, she began plotting her course. She and Mac had come this far. They would see it through to the end.

She wasn't going to kill herself racing a thousand miles to Melbourne in one day. Two would be good enough.

They would be long days on the road. Sleep had to be her first priority. She couldn't waste the rest of the night fretting over her situation. Booze wasn't an option and she didn't have any sleeping pills.

Kate downloaded *The Gunslinger*, the first book in Stephen King's *Dark Tower* saga. She went back to bed with Mac, plugged in her earbuds, and fell asleep listening to the narration.

Mac shook her out of a deep sleep. He grumbled, "I trie' ta take ma medic'ne. I couldn'."

She pushed into a sitting position and removed the earbuds. Swiveling around, she sat next to him on the edge of the bed and wrapped her arms around him. She kissed him. "Okay, honey. It's my fault. I slept through my alarm."

"You been killin' yourself. Needda day off. I shoul' take care uh myself."

Her first day as his wife, and she had already screwed up. Kate looked around the cabin. Pills were scattered about on the floor. Pill bottles lay on their sides on the counter by the sink. Mac had been unable to get one pill out of a bottle and into his mouth. But he didn't stop after the first failure. He went through every one of his medicines.

"Were you able to take any of the pills?"

"I too'em all. Bu' some spill," he said ruefully.

"Did you get the right doses?"

"Tin' so."

She squeezed their heads together and gave him a peck on the cheek. "Okay. We'll write this one off. It won't kill you. We'll get some pill organizers so you can do it yourself."

He gave her a grim look and shook his head. He had spent a lifetime taking care of everything and everybody. Now he couldn't handle the simplest tasks. Kate slid off the bed. "Are you ready for some breakfast?"

Mac pulled her back for a hug and a kiss. Kate cleaned up the pills and cooked eggs while the bread was toasting. A call to Junior was overdue. She wasn't ready for that conversation. They wouldn't make it to Melbourne for another couple of days. He wasn't going to be happy about that.

There was no point in calling him before she had worked out all the details. Mac's meds couldn't be recovered. He needed a new batch. That meant a trip to St. Elizabeth's. Kate was deciding where to lay over at the end of day one when a call from Jimmy interrupted her. He wanted to know how they were doing. She gave him a quick rundown. He said, "Why don't you take the rest of the day off? You haven't visited the Gateway Arch, have you?"

"No," she said, shaking her head for emphasis. "We rushed out of town the last time we were here."

"Okay. I'll clear my calendar and pick you up in an hour."

The afternoon was grand. They started with a riverboat cruise. "The city certainly looks different from here," Kate observed.

Jimmy nodded. "At one time this is what greeted visitors. Now it's a tourist attraction." He added, "And like most people, you only check out tourist attractions when you have company from out of town."

Kate opposed a trip to the top of the arch. They would have to negotiate six flights of stairs going up and coming down. And there wouldn't be any place for Mac to sit once they got up there. He believed he could handle it. He believed he could still do anything he put his mind to. The argument ended on a technicality. The tram was sold out for the rest of the day.

The trio wandered through six themed exhibit areas that portrayed a history of America. The story began just before the revolutionary war and ended as the Vietnam War was heating up. It emphasized American pioneers expanding the nation's borders westward and creating a country that claimed all the territory from the Atlantic to the Pacific. Mac bristled at the idea of Manifest Destiny even though the Scots, Irish and Scots-Irish had been eager participants in the enterprise. He wondered aloud, "Shou' we be cel'brat'n' dat?"

"I can argue either side," Jimmy said. He grinned. "Which do you want?"

Mac turned to the lawyer and shook his head disapprovingly. Jimmy said, "In some instances, at least, authorized representatives of the United States government made legal and binding agreements with representatives of the tribal peoples. However, our government failed to enforce those agreements. The European takeover of the Americas was an atrocity."

Mac stared at the younger man. The lawyer sounded sincere, but the old man couldn't help feeling he was putting them on. Kate broke the silence. "What's the other side?"

"It's not a legal issue. No individual or group gets absolute ownership of property. You own what you can defend. For ten thousand years, Asian settlers in America were protected from the rest of the world by two oceans. They were unprepared for developments when that protection broke down and Europeans landed on their shores. The newly formed U.S. government had little control over its citizens. So, the sides fought it out."

"Wazn' a fair figh'," Mac grumbled.

Kate glared at Jimmy. "We negotiated treaties with the Native Americans and then ignored them."

He shrugged. He had known she wouldn't like his answer. He had also known she wouldn't let it go until she got that answer.

When Mac and Kate were alone again in the RV, she told him she had to call Junior and let him know what was going on. Mac nodded. "You'd li' ta stay here."

"I'm happy here. But keeping you here would be a bad decision. I'd regret it the rest of my life."

"Why? It's nah a ba' place 'n' you gah frenns."

"What about Ann?"

Mac sat staring vacantly, hands folded in his lap. He nodded slowly. "Yeah. You're righ'. We gotta go t' Melbourne."

She placed the call. "Hi, Don. This is Kate."

"Where are you?"

"St. Louis…"

"What the fuck are you doing there?" He demanded. "You're supposed to be bringing my dad down here."

"That's what I'm doing," Kate assured him. "Your father wanted to stop in St. Louis."

"You were supposed to be here a week ago."

"We couldn't fly. I couldn't put him on an airplane."

"How did you get to St. Louis?"

"I drove our camper. He has a bed where he can rest comfortably. And I can give him physical therapy."

"But you're in St. Louis. Isn't that where you wanted to take him in the first place?"

"We stopped over on our way to Melbourne. We'll be there the day after tomorrow."

"Why don't you fly down?"

"That would save a day at most. I promise we'll be down there the day after tomorrow."

"What is it? An hour? Two hours?" He roared. "You could get down here tonight."

"I don't think so," Kate countered. "We don't have tickets. We don't even have reservations." She took a breath. "If we did manage to get seats, it would be on a late flight. That's too much stress for your father. The best we could do is mid-day tomorrow."

Junior insisted, "Get him down here tomorrow."

Kate shook her head in frustration. "I'm going to use my best judgment." Mac was beckoning for the phone. She nodded and said, "Your father is anxious to see Ann, but I need to keep him on schedule. We'll be there the day after tomorrow."

"Shit," Junior growled. "I'm going to have somebody look into how you've been handling things."

"Your father wants to talk to you. I'm turning the phone over to him."

"Hi, son. How are ya?" Mac sounded close to normal.

Junior said something, and Mac responded, "I was in ba' shape las' week. Doc'rs sai' I almos' die'."

Mac kept his eyes on Kate while he listened. He was smiling. "I'm doin' much better. I wen' sigh'seein' t'day."

He frowned. "I wanna stop here," he explained. "Binna rough trip. Kay's doin'all da drivin'. She needda break."

He shook his head as his lips pressed into a thin line. "I don' wanna mess wi' airports. Kay says we'll be in Melbourne da day affer t'morrow." Mac sucked in a deep breath and let it out. "Dat's when we'll dri' upta yer fron' door."

He continued scowling and shaking his head. "How's Ann?"

The answer brought a smile to his face. "Goo'. We'll drop by ta see her soon as we ge' dere."

Mac looked down at the floor and nodded as he listened to Junior. He looked up at Kate and bit his lower lip. "One thin'," He paused for a beat or two. "We gah marrie' yest'day."

His head jerked back at the response. He studied the ceiling as he waited for the rant to finish.

"She makes me happy," He growled. "I gah m' life ta live, boy. 'I may be ol', bu' I'm nah dea'.' Leas' nah yet."

34

Kate got Mac up for his meds and physical therapy at 4. A couple of hours later, they crossed
the Mississippi on their way to Chattanooga,
Tennessee.

Their route took them through Illinois, an iconic
Midwestern state with big cities like Chicago, lots of
farms, rolling hills and woodlands. It had been under-
water a few hundred million years ago. Then it was
a swampland like the Mississippi delta. Ice ages created glaciers that slid down from the north. When the
world warmed, those glaciers melted, leaving behind
tons of sludge that formed rolling hills and fertile
farmland.

Mammoths, mastodons, and other megafauna
still lived in the area when the Asian settlers, the First
Americans, arrived at the end of the last ice age. A
few thousand years later, humans had taken over and
the megafauna were gone. It was still a primitive wilderness when European settlers moved in, clearing
trees, setting up farms and building cities.

An hour east of St. Louis, Kate circled Mt. Vernon and picked up I-57 South. About an hour later, she turned onto I-24, heading southeast toward Nashville. They reached Music City in time for Mac's meds. Kate wanted to kill a couple of hours. She suggested they see the sights.

Mac wasn't interested. The music meant nothing to him. He had never seen or even heard a broadcast of the Grand Ole Opry.

They settled for a visit to Centennial Park, which featured a full-scale replica of the Parthenon. The day was perfect for a walk. Sunny and breezy. Taylor Swift was on endless repeat in Kate's head: *Green was the grass in Centennial Park.* Mac was in a dark mood. Finally, she asked, "Are you going to tell me what's bothering you?"

"Can' b'lieve we're 'lated."

Kate scowled and shook her head. "What?"

"Hard ta b'lieve."

"What's hard to believe?"

"Hunner' years black slaves work dis lan'." Mac sucked in a breath. "Affer da war, blacks couldn' se' foo' in da par'"

"Your relatives?"

"We're all 'lated. Scots. Brits. Ev'n da Irish."

"But not the MacGregors."

"Why nah?" Mac shrugged. "Dey sto' cattle."

Kate shuddered. She gave her brain back to the Country Queen and her thoughts on serendipity. Mac couldn't get past that one wrong-headed choice. They finished their walk in silence.

Back in the RV, they paused next to the kitchenette. The cockpit to their right. Mac's bed to the left. Kate hugged him and breathed, "Mac."

He squeezed her close and kissed her on the forehead. She said, "We can't change the past."

"I know."

"All we can do is work toward a better tomorrow."

"I'm nah sure we're head' dat way."

They kissed. She pulled free. "Go lie down. I've got to get us to Macon."

Kate followed I-24 out of the Nashville Basin into Tennessee's eastern highlands, crossing the Cumberland Plateau and the Appalachians for the next few hours. At Chattanooga, they turned south into Georgia on I-75. Kate stopped for gas and a stretch break - extra vehicular activity - before they reached the greater Atlanta metropolitan area.

Atlanta started out as a railroad depot in the southern foothills of the Appalachian Mountains. It grew into a major transportation hub, making it a valuable asset for the Confederacy. Sherman burned it to the ground in 1864. It was immediately rebuilt and has continued to grow ever since.

The city was not that large, but the suburbs made it the ninth-largest metropolitan area in the country. Atlanta's economy was the tenth largest in the United States. It ranked in the top twenty worldwide.

Kate reached the outer suburbs and made it through the urban sprawl before the evening rush became a problem. Mac's meds were overdue by the time she got them settled in the RV park for the night.

In the morning, Mac watched Kate struggle. She was taking care of everything but she was going through the routines on autopilot.

The problem in marriage, according to Nietzsche, is a lack of friendship. Lovers grope in the dark. Friends see each other in the bright light of day. Mac had slept soundly. Some of his meds made sure of that. But he could see that Kate was not sleeping well.

When she served their eggs, he stood and pulled her into his arms. "It'll be okay. We can hannle i'."

She pressed against him. "I know."

"I bin da new guy. Iz scary."

"Why's this so damn scary? They can't fire me."

Mac chuckled and kissed her on the cheek. "Nah." He pulled back and looked into her eyes. "You da mos' emport'n' person in da worl' ta me."

Kate buried her head in his chest. Mac stroked her hair. "If dey don' like you. We go ba' ta Sain' Loous."

She straightened to look him in the eye. "It's going to work." She gave a slight, sad smile. "We'll make it work."

They stopped for a break outside of Gainesville around 10. Meds, coffee, and a bear claw. Then a short walk around the parking lot. Kate filled the tank and got them back on the road. They were about three hours from Junior's place.

At 1:40, they pulled up to a large two-story ranch-style home set toward the back of a magnificent lawn. Kate paused to study the immaculately manicured grass. A man stood at the edge of the porch, and watched her park the RV. The resemblance was striking, even from that distance.

Kate positioned herself by the camper's door to steady Mac when he lowered himself to the ground. He had taken to backing slowly down the steps holding on for support as he negotiated that last big drop. The procedure was challenging despite repeated practice runs.

A whiff of Old Spice caught Kate's attention. She turned to find Junior standing at her left elbow. He was taller and broader than Mac, but the father-son connection was easy to spot.

The look on his face said everything. He finally had an inkling of his father's condition, and it shook him to the core.

Mac straightened, adjusted his crutches and turned to face his son. He beamed. "Tole ya we'd be here."

Don Junior stepped forward and threw his arms around his father. "You did, Dad. You did."

"Can we go inside?" Kate asked. The blazing equatorial sun was scalding her skin in spite of a gentle ocean breeze. And she felt awkward. She had considered getting back in the camper and taking a nap while the two men got re-acquainted.

Junior greeted her with a condescending smile. He nodded and grabbed Mac's elbow. "C'mon."

The old man pushed his son away and started toward the house. The younger man fell in step. Kate closed the camper door and followed.

As they neared the porch, Junior broke rank and hustled ahead to open the door. Once inside, he had to bring a chair from the kitchen for his father because the living room furniture was too low and soft. He moved with the grace and ease of an athlete. It looked like he had put on a few pounds, but Kate was certain he worked to keep himself in shape.

Air-conditioning made the living room an oasis. A sixty-inch TV dominated one wall. A large leather sectional was set against the stairwell that led from the entrance to the second floor. Two matching leather chairs sat in front of a picture window that looked out onto the front lawn.

"When did this happen?" Junior asked as he held the chair for his father.

"I don' know." Mac shook his head. "Had a stroke in Fairbanks." He sucked in a breath. "Bu' I was havin' headaches 'n' stumble' a couplla time'. Yer mom 'sisted I see a docker."

"Mom knew about this?"

"Nah sure. She die'." Mac closed his eyes and shuddered. "We were takin' a na'. I woke up. She didn' look right. Call her name. Didn' answer. I check. I knew she was dea', soon as I touch' her."

Junior nodded. He'd heard the story before. Mac was looking at the floor, but his eyes were shut. He shook his head. "I got ba' to da docker affer da funeral." He focused a hard stare on his son. "He tole me I had a tumor on ma brain. Didn' loo' good. Rex was kill'. Hi'by a truck."

The pain in his voice was too much for Kate. She wanted to run over and hold him.

"Why didn't you tell us?" his son pressed.

"I though' you didn' care. I took care of thing' like I done all ma life."

Junior's mouth dropped open. His brows arched. He shook his head. "That's not true."

"You pai' yer respecks 'n' lef'."

Junior bit his lip and dropped his head. He looked up to face his dad. "I'm sorry. I had to be at the office. I could only afford to take off a couple of days. We stayed in a hotel because there wasn't enough room for all of us at the house." He grimaced and shook his head. "When we tried to talk to you, you acted like you didn't want company." He ran a hand through what was left of his hair. "I'm sorry. I didn't mean to hurt you. I just didn't know what to do."

Mac shrugged. "I gah more 'pinions. More tes's." He looked up at the ceiling and breathed out heavily. "I cou' drah dead any time. Trea'men' mi' gimme a year." He bit on his lower lip. "Foun' a docker prescribe meds ta ease da symp'ms. He tole me I ha' 6 munns. I ma'a will. You 'n' Ann are okay. I sol' da house. I bough' da RV 'n' start' 'cross da counnry."

"And now you've got a new wife," Junior chided. There was a sarcastic bite in his voice. "How does she fit into all of this?"

"I meh Kay in Sain' Loous. She convince' me I shouldn' be drivin' alone. She offer' to go alon' 'n' hel'."

"So just like that. She jumps in and gets you all to herself. Do you realize the ethical implications of what she did?"

Kate could feel her cheeks burning. "I don' givva damn," Mac snarled. "'n' I hope you never say anythin' like dat again."

"I'm sorry, Dad. But we have to be realistic. She took advantage of you. I'll bet she stands to get a substantial inheritance."

Kate was ready to explode. Her fingernails dug into her palms. She wanted to run from the house before she strangled Junior. "Where were you when I nee' some'ody?" Mac demanded with a quiet fury.

"You could have told me what was going on," Junior shot back.

Mac turned on his son in a rage. His mouth clamped shut as his eyes bulged and his face reddened. "You couldda ask'," he snarled. Kate was afraid he was about to have a stroke. He took a deep breath to calm himself and shook his head. "You gonna tell me you wouldda dropp' everythin' 'n' come wi' me across da counnry?"

"I would have moved you down here where Ann and I could take care of you."

"But you wouldnna join' me on da trip."

Junior clamped his hands to his head and looked up at the ceiling. "What difference would that have made, Dad?"

Mac took some time before answering. "Diff'r'nce 'tween livin' 'n' rottin' away."

Kate could see Junior's dilemma. A career and a growing family were enough to challenge anybody's energy and resources. When you're busting your butt to succeed, it's difficult to imagine having no challenges to tackle. For a man in his peak years aging is a fuzzy, far-off reality. But the pointless, dead-end argument had to be stopped before it brought on a stroke. Besides, she was supposed to get Mac to the hospital for a visit with his daughter. Time to get the show on the road. She stood, put her hands on her hips and stretched her back. "Your father wants to see Ann this afternoon. Can we do that?"

Junior fixed her with an icy stare. "I need to give her a heads up. I haven't had a chance to tell her about the marriage."

Kate nodded. "Okay. Would you give her a call? We don't want to miss visiting hours."

Junior rose from his chair and pulled car keys from his pocket. He threw them to Kate. "Go ahead and get in the car. I'll be right out."

35

Kate was bringing a folded wheelchair from the RV for Mac when Junior stepped out onto the porch. He stopped to watch. "What's that?"

"A wheelchair. We got it when we were sightseeing in St. Louis. Your father needs it."

"He walked up to the house."

"I'm pretty sure the hospital will be more challenging."

Mac yelled from the front passenger seat, "I tol' her I didn' need it."

Junior lifted his hands, smiled, and shook his head. Kate said, "I'm bringing it just in case."

He met her at the back of his Lexus and held out a hand. She gave him the keys. He popped the trunk open with the press of a button and loaded the wheelchair. Then, with an exasperated shake of his head, he marched to his seat behind the wheel.

Kate closed Mac's door and got in the back. Junior hadn't started the engine. He was still processing the situation. His eyes came to rest on the shell of a man sitting next to him. His father, who had always been healthy and energetic, was suddenly decrepit. Then he turned to study the woman climbing into the rear seat and buckling up. The old man's new wife was a piece of work. Something would have to be done about her. But what?

When they reached the hospital parking lot, Junior went straight to the handicapped parking near the entrance. All the slots were occupied. He grumbled, "Suddenly everybody in Florida is handicapped."

"A lot of elderly people move here," Kate observed.

"Then they should put in more spaces."

"You can't legally use them. You don't have a permit."

"My father is disabled," Junior objected.

"He still needs a permit," Kate retorted.

Junior turned to glare at her before setting off to find a parking space he could use. He cruised the aisles until he found one in a far corner of the lot.

The men got out of the car and studied the situation. The hospital entrance was a quarter-mile away. Kate set up the wheelchair. Mac gave a disgusted shake of his head and surrendered. He sat for his ride across the lot.

Junior pushed. Kate followed with the crutches. On the ride up to Ann's floor, Mac insisted he would walk to his daughter's room on his own. When they got out of the elevator, he took the crutches from Kate. Junior handed her the wheelchair. She reached the doorway of Ann's room just in time to hear, "Dad, it's so good of you to come."

"It too' a while," Mac rumbled, "but I ha' ta ma' sure you're okay."

Kate parked the wheelchair in the hall and squeezed into the crowded room.

Ann was sitting on the edge of her bed. Her left arm in a sling. Half her face swathed in bandages. But she was exuberant. She held out her good arm as her father hobbled over for a hug. Her good eye flickered in Kate's direction just long enough for a quick assessment.

"Junyer sai' yer bandages were comin' off," Mac ventured after they had hugged. He sounded disappointed.

"They could have," Anne said. "But my face is hideous. I asked them to wait until tomorrow." She squeezed his face against hers and kissed him. As he straightened, her right hand caught his head and explored his bandage. "I'm so sorry I wasn't there for you," she said in a barely audible voice. Then pushing him away, she chided gaily, "Aren't you going to introduce your new wife?"

Mac maneuvered around to face Kate. "Come'ere, 'oney." He nodded toward Ann. "My daught'r." He jerked his head toward Junior and said, "'n' you meh my so'."

He waited as Kate made her way to his side. He pecked her on the cheek. "Ev'ryone, dis ma bri', Katrin Grah'm MuhGregor."

Ann extended a hand. "Very nice to meet you, Katherine." She took the measure of her father's child bride as they shook hands. "Or should I call you

Mom?" She purred and winked. There was no mistaking the snark.

"I prefer Kate."

"Welcome to the family, Kate." Ann said in a cheery voice laced with acid. "Dad picked a winner. Didn't he, Don?"

Junior grimaced. "Dad said he only has a few months to live. He might drop dead at any time."

Ann recoiled. Her eyes narrowed as she studied her father. "What's going on, Dad?"

"I gah brain cancer. Stage four." He smiled at his daughter and nodded. "You can live a cuppla years 'less you're ov'r sevenny."

"Isn't there something you can do?" she pressed.

"Yeah. Bu' it's worse 'n dyin'. I'm gonna make da mos' udda time I gah lef'."

"You said your doctor gave you some medication," Junior interjected.

Mac nodded. "Mos'ly for da pain. 'n' for da tumor." He chuckled. "Dat don' work."

Ann said, "Kate doesn't have any place to sit. Why don't we go to the solarium?" She slid to the floor and into her slippers.

Junior scowled in Kate's direction. His lip curled slightly. His nose scrunched. He nodded. "Sounds like a good idea."

Ann squeezed Kate's arm and gave her a sisterly kiss as she sailed into the hallway. Mac followed her, and Junior stepped in behind him. Kate grabbed the wheelchair and trailed after them.

When she reached the bright, spacious visiting area, Mac was looking around for a place to sit. The hospital had provided lounge chairs. They were comfortable but they weren't suitable for an elderly, handicapped man. Mac couldn't have gotten up again without help. Kate pushed the wheelchair over and tugged on his sleeve. When he looked at her, she indicated the seat with a nod. He glowered but plopped into the chair. She kissed him on the cheek.

Junior picked up the conversation. "What happened in Fairbanks?"

Mac looked puzzled. Junior rephrased his question. "When you were hospitalized in Fairbanks, what happened?"

"Dey hadda r'move da tum'r. Said i' was killin' me" Mac paused to smile at Kate. "Gave me more time."

"Why didn't you get it taken care of while you were in the hospital up there?"

Mac grinned. "You don' get it. Can' ta' care of it. Dey remove da tumor. It grow ba'. Dey zap it. Fee' me poison ta kill it." Mac had to pause to catch his breath. "It jus' come ba'. Spendda ressa ma life in da hospital." He looked at Ann. "My girl was in da hospital. I hadda come see 'er."

That speech took the air out of the room. Kate couldn't get out of there fast enough. Mac sensed her shifting her weight from one foot to the other as she stood behind him. He squeezed her hand. Then he asked, "Wha' happ'n' ta yer face?"

Ann said, "I was T-boned. The airbags saved me, but splinters of glass cut my face up pretty bad."

"Can dey fix i'?"

"It'll heal. They're applying creams to minimize the scarring. I should be able to cover the remaining damage with makeup."

Ann turned her good eye on Kate. "Aren't you a little old for this sort of thing, Dad?" She paused expectantly. "She's not much older than your granddaughter."

"Wha's age gotta do wid i'?" Mac growled.

"Sex for one thing."

"We're okay," Mac assured her. "She's pregnan'."

Kate needed a place to hide. She wanted to strangle him, but she didn't have any rope. Junior's jaw dropped open. He wanted to say, "*You already have children.*" Ann gasped, "You're pregnant?"

Kate nodded. "How did that happen?" Ann demanded.

"We ma' love," Mac crowed.

Ann's good eye popped open. A hundred snappy responses raced through her brain before she managed, "Oh. Okay. Congratulations."

Junior looked at his watch. "It's getting late. Ann needs to get her rest. Why don't we come back tomorrow?"

Mac scowled. He reached over and took his daughter's hand. "We' be back t'morrow, 'oney."

"That sounds good," she said with a perfunctory smile. "Give me some time to get the bandages off."

Halfway to the door, Junior stopped and turned back. "Give me a call when you're ready, and I'll bring them back."

He walked out, leaving Kate to push Mac back to the car. Ann came over and hugged her new "mother". "I'm sorry. That was just such a shock. I'm really happy for you and dad."

Kate returned the embrace. "Thank you."

After an awkward pause, she pushed Mac out of the room without looking back.

36

Kate got them set up in a mobile home park not far from the ocean. She bought a car from one of those places that buys and sells used cars. She figured she could sell it back to them when and if she decided to move out of town.

Don Junior called his dad a few times. He never came for a visit. He and Ann did consult with Kate about getting a private duty nurse to help take care of their dad. But the effort lost momentum and evaporated. Kate felt sure they preferred to leave the job to her. She was working for free and if something happened to her, they could put him in a nursing home.

Kate was in a difficult position. She would never abandon Mac, but the lifestyle was stifling. She had little to do. None of it challenging. And no human contact except for her husband.

Mac wanted her to get a job. He knew she needed something to live for. An opportunity to put her talent and training to use. And the company of others. He insisted he would be fine by himself. All he needed was a medical alert system for emergencies.

Kate looked into a few openings. Both sides had issues. She knew someone would have to take care of Mac while she was at work, and that would eat up her salary. She was pregnant. That never came up in an interview, but Kate suspected no one wanted to hire a pregnant woman who would be taking family leave as soon as she started working.

The couple talked about going back to St. Louis. Mac had said that's what they would do if things didn't work out in Melbourne. But the situation wasn't clear-cut. He was happy being near his kids and grandkids, even if they didn't have much time for him. Mac complained about them. He also sympathized with them. He knew from experience what it was like to juggle a full-time job and a family.

Ann made an effort. She came over to stay with her father so Kate could have time to herself. The three of them went to movies at a local theater. She offered the services of her teenage daughter, Betty. But the asking price for those services was $20 an hour. That was steep. Besides, the teen didn't really get along with her grandfather. Mac complained that the girl sat in the cockpit and played with her phone the whole time she was with him. He said, "Whys she cumin ov'r? She can play wi' her phone at home."

They had to live with it once in a while because no one else was available. Ann got Kate into her book club. Kate insisted that Betty stay with Mac while she was at the meetings.

Ann arranged a baby shower a few months after the couple arrived. Kate was flattered but not enthusiastic. She didn't want to leave Mac alone. Mac refused to be stuck with Betty all afternoon, but he wouldn't hear of Kate turning down the invitation. "She tryin' to ma' you pardda da family."

"Who's going to take care of you while I'm away?"

"I be okay forra cuplla hours."

"At least let me get Betty."

"She no help. I be fine. You go ha' fun."

"How am I supposed to have fun while I'm worrying about you here by yourself?"

"I live a lodda years wi'ou' yer help."

"It's different now."

"An' dere's nuddin we can do aboud i'." Mac glared at her. "Le' me hannle thinz. You go ha' fun."

Kate stifled a retort and walked to the cockpit. When she came back, she said, "Okay. But you better be here waiting for me when I get home."

That seemed to settle the argument. On the day of the event, Kate dressed in a white blouse that hung loosely over her black slacks. She had some time to kill. Betty was going to drive her to the shower. She went forward to the cockpit and pulled up Rachmaninoff on her headset. But She got antsy. Kate put the music aside and went back to sit with Mac. "I'm going to call and tell her I don't feel well."

"Ya loo' fine ta me."

"But I'm going to be spending the afternoon with a bunch of strangers."

"I though' dey were yer frienns."

"They're Ann's friends."

"You never meddem?"

"Once or twice at the book club."

Kate's phone rang. Betty was outside waiting for her. Mac said, "I guess you bedder ge' goin'."

She set the phone down on the sink and walked over to kiss him. She sat next to him and stroked his cheek, a rueful look on her face. Betty honked her horn impatiently. Mac gave Kate a slight push. "Go."

She kissed him and raced out to the car. The teenager was chatty and nervous. Chauffeuring an adult was a new gig for her.

Ann and her friends were great. They ate, sipped wine, and talked about Melbourne. Where to shop. Where to dine. What to avoid.

Just as the party was getting good, someone knocked. Ann stood and went to see who was there.

A shiver ran through Kate's body when the door opened. Out of the corner of her eye, she saw a tall, dark woman. Black tresses with streaks of silver cascading over her shoulders. Kate turned to face the stranger. The woman's eyes bore into her soul. She said in a soft contralto, "I must speak with Mrs. MacGregor."

A weird feeling swept over Kate. She was looking down on a roomful of people. The woman at the door said, "Katherine."

Somebody screamed, "No!"

The woman at Kate's feet was shaking her head. Her face buried in her hands.

"Katherine," the thickly accented, contralto voice called again, and Kate found herself sitting on the sofa. Tears streaming down her cheeks. "No," she sobbed.

"Katherine, you must come with me right now."

Kate was too stunned to think coherently. She felt herself stand and walk to the door as if in a trance. Tereza took her hand and pulled gently. "We have to go," she urged.

Kate tagged behind the Gypsy to a Malibu with a dull red finish parked at the curb and allowed herself to be nudged into the passenger seat. She sat in a stupor while Tereza fastened her seat belt. Once they were underway, Kate forced herself to breathe. Tears ran down her cheeks. She wiped them with the backs of her hands. "He'll be so furious when he finds out I cried."

"It's all right," Tereza assured her.

"Is he okay?"

"He's resting peacefully."

"Peacefully?" Kate shrieked. "He's dead. Isn't he?"

"He's at peace. No more suffering. Isn't that what you wanted?"

Kate nodded. "Yes." Then she shook her head. "No. I wanted him to hold his son. That's the one thing that kept him going."

"I'm sorry."

"Why didn't you call and warn me?"

"I was delayed. I called to make sure you were with him, but no one answered."

Kate searched frantically for her phone. It wasn't in her purse. That made no sense. She never left the camper without it. Except this time. She had set it on the counter to say goodbye to Mac after the call from Betty. Then she'd rushed out to the car when the teen started honking.

Kate stared out the window as they rolled through a pleasant neighborhood with trees and manicured lawns hinting of paradise. "I should have been there with him."

"Perhaps it was better that you weren't," Tereza suggested. "If you had been there, you would have moved heaven and earth to save him, and he would have fought to hang on because he loved you so much. This way there was nothing anyone could do about it."

When they reached the camper, Tereza raced to the door to keep Kate from charging in. She held out a hand for the keys, opened the door, and climbed inside. Kate pushed in behind her to get a peek. Mac was a few feet away, sprawled on the floor, staring at her. She shouted, "Mac." and bolted up the steps.

He didn't move. Not even an eyelid. It was a death stare. Kate charged over to him and checked for a pulse. Nothing. No heartbeat. His skin was cold and rubbery. She pushed his lids shut and kissed him on the cheek.

Kate crawled onto his back and wrapped her arms around him. Nothing. The tears started again. Anger began to build. It became a fury that could not be contained. She pounded on his shoulders and raged, "You fucking bastard. You should have let me stay here with you."

Tereza pulled her to her feet. "We have to go back to the car and let the police handle this."

A blinking notification light caught Kate's attention as she staggered out of the RV. Her phone. On the counter by the sink. She guessed Mac had gotten up from the sofa to answer Tereza's call, took a couple of steps, and collapsed. She reached for the phone. Tereza grabbed her wrist and pushed her out of the camper.

The Gypsy called 911 as soon as she had the grieving widow settled in the car. "I just brought my friend home from a party. When we went into her RV, we found her husband lying on the floor."

She shook her head. "No. He isn't moving. He doesn't seem to be breathing."

She nodded as she listened. "I think he may be dead. Please send someone out to check on him."

The ambulance took a while. Kate sat with her face buried in her hands. Elbows digging into her thighs. She relived every detail of her life with him - from their first meeting to their last kiss.

37

A soft tap on the window brought her out of the reverie. A brunette in a blue blazer, white cotton sweater and jeans stood beside the car demanding attention. When the window slid open, she lowered herself to Kate's eye level. Her gray-green eyes were icy pools. "Mrs. MacGregor, I'm detective Lee Bishop," she said. "I know this is a bad time, but I need to ask some questions."

The words made no sense, but Kate nodded and mumbled, "Okay."

"Can you come over to my car? Please?"

The car was a black Chevy Trailblazer. Bishop opened the back door for Kate and climbed in behind her. "This must be quite a shock," she began as she opened a notebook. "I understand you found your husband lying on the floor when you got back from a party."

"Yes. That's correct."

"And Ms. Ivanova brought you back from the party?"

"Yes."

"Was she with you at the party?"

"No. She came to the door and asked for me."

"Are you good friends?"

"I've only talked to her one other time. It was a phone call."

Bishop paused to jot something in her notebook. "But you left a party with her."

"My husband knew her. I trust her." Kate shrugged. "I was afraid something had happened to Mac."

"Why was that?"

"It's the reality I live with. He has – had – stage four brain cancer." Kate turned to face the detective. "I didn't want to go to the party. He insisted."

"He was alone at the time?"

"That's the way he wanted it."

"Sounds careless. Negligent."

"I suppose. Mac knew he was going to die. He refused to let that dictate how he lived. It was like a religion for him."

Bishop shook her head and clamped her lips shut in silent disapproval as she made notes. She looked up, scowling. Kate said, "He knew he wouldn't live forever. He wasn't going to try. He insisted that his last days had to be as normal as possible."

"So, it wasn't a complete shock when you walked in and found him dead?"

"It was a terrible shock. I don't know how you wouldn't be shocked if you found someone you loved lying dead on the floor."

"You're right. Finding a dead body is a shock."

"I have watched many of my patients die. That is not at all like losing someone you love."

"Patients?"

"I'm a nurse. I've worked with elderly patients in a senior care facility for the last ten years."

"Brookdale?"

"No. I'm on a leave of absence from St. Elizabeth's in St. Louis."

"I think you are going to have to elaborate on that."

"It's a long story, and I want to have a lawyer. Can you give me a couple of days to recover and find a lawyer?"

"Why do you need a lawyer?"

"Because you are asking a bunch of questions I'm uncomfortable with."

"I should take you in."

"For what? I didn't do anything."

"What you did put him in danger."

"Is your job dangerous?"

"Sometimes."

"Has that ever made you think about changing careers?"

Bishop shook her head. "You have a wedding band," Kate observed. "Does your husband try to stop you from doing your job?"

"It's not up to him," she huffed. "He knew what I did and what it involved when he married me."

"That's exactly what Mac would say if he could talk right now. He couldn't choose when he would die. But he had the absolute right to choose how he lived."

Kate pushed the door open and walked back to Tereza's car.

38

Kate slumped into the passenger seat and began sobbing. Tereza patted her thigh. "We should get a room. You don't want to sleep here tonight."

"After they leave. I need to get a few things."

An hour later, the police drove off without saying a word. The two women went inside the camper and looked around. Mac's body was gone but everything else seemed to be in place. Kate collected her iPad, phone and the legal papers that justified her actions.

As soon as they were in the room, Kate found a seat and called Jimmy. He said, "I'm so sorry Kate. How are you doing?"

"I'm still numb."

"You're not alone in that camper, are you?"

"No. I'm with a friend. She volunteered to stay with me tonight?"

"Alright. Try to get some rest and let me know if there's anything I can do."

"I think I need a lawyer."

"Why?"

"The police grilled me and searched the camper."

"Probably nothing. But I've got some friends. I'll get one of them to look out for you."

"Thanks."

"Get some rest and call me in the morning."

It was a rough, mostly sleepless night. The District Attorney's Office called Kate first thing in the morning. She told them she would get back to set up an appointment as soon as she arranged for legal counsel.

Tereza insisted they go down to the restaurant for breakfast while they were waiting for Jimmy to start his day. Kate fidgeted through the meal and hurried back to the room to call her cousin. He said, "How are you holding up?"

"As well as can be expected. I guess."

"Is there anything I can do?"

"Put me in touch with a good lawyer."

"David Feinstein, a classmate of mine, is expecting your call. I'll text you the information. Anything else I can do for you?"

"I wish you were here."

"Dave is a great lawyer, and he's well-connected. I would want him handling this even if I was there."

"Okay. I'll talk to you later."

"Is there anybody I should notify?"

"No. I talked to Sam for an hour last night. I'll get in touch with the others after I've had a chance to figure things out."

Dave Feinstein was sympathetic and upbeat. He offered to discuss the case with the DA and schedule a meeting. After that, he would get together with Kate and figure out their strategy.

When Kate sat down with Feinstein in his office, he told her that Donald McGregor Junior had filed a complaint against her. He had alleged the marriage was coerced and therefore invalid. He requested that Ms. Graham be physically separated from his father. Kate's leaving the old man to die alone in the camper underscored her incompetence.

When she got in to see the DA, he opened with, "Why was Mr. McGregor alone in the camper?"

Kate said, "That's the way he wanted it."

"Would you elaborate?"

"His daughter Ann Stillwell arranged a baby shower for me. Mac insisted that I go. He said he didn't need and didn't want a babysitter."

"You have been working as a nurse with elderly patients in a senior care facility for the last 10 years?"

"Yes."

"Didn't it occur to you that someone should be with your husband while you were out for the afternoon?"

"Yes. But I also recognized that he was an adult in full control of his faculties. The decision was up to him."

"With all due respect, he was an elderly brain cancer patient who had suffered two strokes."

"He was also a man who read, went to movies, and exercised regularly."

The DA grimaced and moved on to a new topic. "Why did you marry him?"

"That's what he wanted."

"What about you?"

"I agreed. The second time he asked me."

"The second time?"

"He asked me and I said I didn't think we needed to change our relationship. He pushed. He said I was the most important person in the world to him."

"That was it?"

Kate looked over at Feinstein. He nodded. "He was concerned about my legal status once we reached Melbourne."

"Meaning?"

"I wanted to keep the camper. It's my home but he was the legal owner."

"That's it?"

"I think he wanted to leave me something in his will."

"Because of the baby?"

"He didn't know about that."

"But he set up an annuity for the child."

"That was after we got married. I announced my pregnancy after the ceremony."

"Did he change his will once or twice?"

"I'm not sure. He and Jimmy discussed it while we were sightseeing in St. Louis. Later that night Jimmy and his secretary came by the camper. Mac signed the will, the secretary and I witnessed it, and she notarized it."

The question-and-answer session continued for another 20 minutes. Feinstein gave the DA a copy of the agreements between Mac and Kate. They stipulated that Kate could not provide medical treatment because she was not a doctor. Her only obligation was to do her best to get him medical care in the event of an emergency. There was no emergency at the time she left for the baby shower.

The DA told Kate not to leave town until the matter was resolved.

She powered on her phone when she got back to the camper. A long list of missed calls and messages needed her attention. She responded to some of them. Gert Williams assured her that her job would be waiting whenever she wanted to go back to work. Ann Stillwell was sympathetic but said her brother Don had requested an autopsy. That would take a couple of weeks. Ann said she had contacted the cemetery in Annapolis about burying her father in the grave next to her mother.

Kate put down the phone and raged at the high-handed behavior. Tereza listened with a bemused smile. "What difference does it make where they bury him?"

"He's my husband."

"Where do you want him buried?"

"I don't know. I haven't thought about it."

"You won't take his body to St. Louis without a big fight," Tereza pointed out. "Do you want to be buried in Melbourne?"

Kate turned and stared in shock. The Gypsy continued, "He will be with you the rest of your life no matter where they bury his body."

"I know, but a husband and wife are supposed to be buried together."

"He's also Anne's husband."

"Was," Kate pouted.

Tereza closed her eyes and breathed calmly. "I see your remains in an urn on your son's mantle."

"Really?"

"This is not guaranteed. But what happens to your remains will be more important to him than to you."

Tereza walked over to her young friend and pulled her into an embrace. She whispered in her husky voice, "Mac will be laid to rest. It does not matter where. He lives on in you. Focus on what matters – your son."

Legal challenges hijacked Kate's focus in the weeks following her husband's death. A series of virtual hearings collected testimony in the matter of Don Junior's challenge to his father's marriage. The judge and lawyers for both parties sat through Zoom sessions with witnesses who had interacted with the couple while they were in St. Louis. The judge concluded there was no basis for a challenge. The marriage was valid.

That resolved another matter. Mac had set up a joint bank account so Kate would have money while they were in Melbourne. Junior wanted a judge to freeze the account until questions about his father's death were fully resolved. Once the marriage was declared valid, any basis for freezing the account went away. The money was Kate's to use as she saw fit.

The DA was still pursuing a negligence charge. He brought Kate in for another interview. He wanted to know how a middle-aged nurse got involved with the elderly Mr. MacGregor.

"He invited me to sit with him while he ate dinner. We topped it off with pie and coffee. He told me about this trip to meet his cousin in Alaska," Kate said. "I could see that he was not well, and I was concerned about him driving like that."

"Why did that concern you?"

"As I said, he didn't look well. I was afraid he would have a heart attack or stroke while he was cruising along on a busy interstate."

"That's it? You were worried he'd cause an accident on a freeway?"

"That and I was bored. The idea of going places I had never been before appealed to me."

"Did he pay you to travel with him?"

"I was going to take off work for a short time, so I negotiated a stipend. My cousin, Jimmy Smith, drew up the contract."

"Did that contract give you the right to make legal and medical decisions on Mr. MacGregor's behalf?"

"Yes, sir."

"The two of you were alone on the road for several weeks. Eventually, you were able to convince your elderly client to marry you and change his will to include you and your unborn child."

"No, sir. I told him not to change his will. I was against marrying him because I didn't want to end up in a court battle with his children."

"What made you change your mind?"

"He was hurt when I turned him down."

"Was he concerned about the well-being of the child you were carrying?"

"He didn't know about that."

"But he set up an annuity for the child and one for you."

"I told him about the baby after we were married. He worked out the financial arrangements with Jimmy the next day."

The prosecutor was skeptical, but he had another resource, a tie-breaker. He called his sister, a nationally recognized expert on the care of cancer patients. She and Kate went over everything in a wide-ranging discussion that lasted a little over an hour. When the sister broke off the meeting because of another appointment, she closed with, "Bob, Mr. MacGregor had a stage 4 glioblastoma, which meant he had months to live. The only thing you can do for someone in that situation is give them emotional support."

"Does that include engaging in sexual intercourse?"

"It's not that simple. Many people are forced into the role of caregiver when their significant other is diagnosed with cancer. They have to work out a way to merge the two roles."

"As I understand it she had sex with him before they got married."

"Mrs. MacGregor's behavior raises ethical issues, but our highest responsibility is taking care of the patient's needs. Love is something we all need."

"She took advantage of a sick, elderly man."

"They were two people on a cross-country vacation. One of them had brain cancer. No law says you have to stop living just because you're dying from brain cancer."

The DA watched his sister with a poker face. He said, "The ethics of her behavior don't bother you?"

"If I found myself falling in love with a dying patient, my instinct would be to turn him over to others so I could be there for him. I don't know what I would do in Kate's situation where no one else was available. I can't fault her. I might recommend her for a medal."

"Why wasn't he in a hospital where he could be given proper care?"

"It looks like he refused medical treatment. That isn't common, but it isn't unheard of. I'll follow up with the doctors he saw."

The negligence charges were dropped. But Kate had no doubt she would still have to answer for her actions when she returned to St. Elizabeth's.

Waiting for the autopsy results was the worst part for Kate. Friends got her through the ordeal. Sam Reinhart called her or she called him just to talk every day or so. Rabbi Zenman, who had officiated at the wedding, called to make sure she was okay. Eddie Flores called a couple of times. Tereza assured her there was nothing to worry about. "They will find that he died of natural causes. What else could they find?"

"That I was negligent. That I should've done more to keep him alive."

The Gypsy's smiled dismissively and shook her head. "Others could have done more to keep him breathing. No one could have done more to keep him alive."

David Feinstein and Jimmy Smith took on the legal battles critical to Kate's survival. When Don and Ann threatened to challenge the will, Feinstein met with their attorney. "If that will is changed, it will be in my client's favor. Florida has adopted the Uniform Disposition of Community Property Rights at Death Act. It will be up to the judge to decide on equitable distribution. The key consideration will be her status as Mr. McGregor's wife with a child on the way."

The challenge to the will evaporated.

As predicted, the autopsy determined that Mac died of natural causes.

A viewing was held two days after the autopsy results were announced. Friends turned out to support Junior and his sister. They had little interest in Kate. She was an interloper. A gold digger. She had gotten pregnant and forced the old man to marry her.

Kate left early and found a church where she could sit and meditate. She was not a religious person, even though she had been raised Catholic. But thinking about Jesus and his trials helped her come to terms with her own situation.

Mac's body was transported to Annapolis for burial in the plot next to his wife of 40 years. Tereza accompanied Kate to Annapolis for the burial. Family friends who showed up huddled near Junior and Anne, ignoring the two women. It may not have been a conscious decision. Anne's children had once been part of the community. They had buried their mother last year. Now they were burying their father. Kate was a stranger, not a welcome guest.

She walked over to throw a handful of dirt on the casket. Looking down for her last goodbye, she realized a part of her was with him and a part of him was inextricably woven into her being.

39

After the funeral, Tereza announced that she had to get back to her life in Parkersburg. Kate had loose ends to tie up in Melbourne. Taking care of Mac's will was simple. He had disposed of most of his property before setting out on his journey. She inherited the rest. Ann and Don Junior each got a check. Dave Feinstein helped her with legal documents that had to be filed. She sold her car back to the dealership that had sold it to her. The RV Park kept her deposit.

Kate made a few calls to let friends in St. Louis know when to expect her. Goodbye and good riddance to Melbourne. She detoured north for an overnight stop in Annapolis and a final visit to Mac's grave. Then she set off for home, retracing the route that had brought him into her life.

Tereza joined her for lunch at the dilapidated but neighborly My Country Kitchen. They didn't have much to say. Kate wanted to thank the woman for her help and support. The Gypsy assured her the future was bright. "Two paths beckon. I feel your past pulling very strongly. You can return to the old comfortable life. I do not believe that is the road you were meant to travel. This is an opportunity for you to follow your true calling."

"I've been thinking about that. I want to finish my nursing studies. But I have a child on the way."

"And Mac spoiled you," Tereza observed. "You are not ready to be alone."

"That's the worst part. I knew he was going to die. I didn't expect to feel lost and empty."

"You did not expect to fall in love when you met him. These things take time."

"How long?"

"How should I know?"

"You're psychic," Kate snapped. "You see things."

Tereza's lip curled into a skeptical smile. She made her young friend wait. "What I see is a warrior. A knight. Sir Galahad perhaps. A woman could not ask for a better companion on her journey."

Kate gasped. Her mouth hung open. "Eddie?" was on the tip of her tongue, but she couldn't say the name aloud. Tereza stood, pulled a twenty from her wallet and dropped it on the table. "I must go now. Your future is in your hands. Do not waste this opportunity. Drive forward. That is what you do best."

Kate made it across Ohio and into Indiana before stopping for gas. She pulled alongside the pumps in a convenience store parking lot. She was about to get out and fill the tank when she realized the storefront was boarded over. Panic and terror seized her. She sat frozen. Unable to stand. A soft rap on her window brought her back. An African American man signaled for her to open the window. "Excuse me," he said. "Where did you get this camper?"

Kate stared at him. He asked, "Ma'am, are you alright?"

"Yes, I think so. Can you tell me something?"

He nodded. She asked, "What happened to that window?"

He turned to look. After a long, thoughtful pause, he answered, "It was broken during a robbery. They haven't gotten around to replacing it."

Another wave of anxiety hit Kate. She swallowed. "The camper belonged to my husband."

"Oh," he said. "I apologize for the intrusion. It looks like the one a friend of mine drove."

On a whim, Kate said, "That was my husband, Tim."

His eyes narrowed to a squint. He slowly shook his head. "I don't think my friend was married. He was alone."

"We didn't meet until after the robbery."

"He had brain cancer. Right?"

"Yes."

"Is that why he isn't with you?"

"Yes."

Tim looked down. When he looked up, there was a sad smile on his face. "I'm sorry for your loss."

Kate got out and walked around to him. They hugged. She said, "Thank you for taking care of him."

He stepped back and shrugged. "Is that a baby bump?"

"Yes. I'm pregnant."

"Sheeeit. He was something else."

Kate laughed. "Definitely."

She inserted a credit card to pay for the gas. Tim grabbed the nozzle. "Let me do that."

After he returned the nozzle to its slot, she hugged him and kissed him. "Are you okay?"

"I am blessed," he said emphatically.

"Are they still after you about the robbery?"

"I'm black. They're always after me about something." He sighed and shook his head. "They aren't pursuing that, but they are keeping an eye on me."

"I'm sorry. It shouldn't be that way."

He looked at her impassively. Her cheeks flushed. *Pathetic, stupid thing to say*. She wanted to crawl into the nearest hole. Instead, she hugged him and kissed him again. He kissed her back. "Take care of yourself."

That was Kate's cue. She climbed back into the captain's chair and took off for St. Louis.

Six hours later, she pulled into Camp Discovery. A man sat on the front porch outside the office. He was barely visible in the twilight, but she knew who it was. She stopped. He ambled over and climbed into the camper. Eddie Flores flopped into the passenger seat. "Welcome back."

Kate said, "I want to stay here with my camper until I get things straightened out."

"We can take care of that tomorrow," he chuckled. "Have you had anything to eat?"

"I've been snacking all day."

"Let me take you to Sam's for a real meal."

Sweet. Thoughtful. was Kate's first reaction. Then *Chivalrous.* The Gypsy's words flashed through her mind. She looked at her companion and saw him for the first time. No knight in shining armor. He wore a dirty T-shirt, jeans and jungle mocs, the clothes of a working man. But Sir Galahad had nothing on him. He'd been a warrior. He'd told her about a battle with the Taliban in the Afghan mountains. It made The Gunfight at the O.K. Corral sound like a schoolyard dustup.

A slight movement brought her back to the moment. He had tilted his head and was looking for an answer. Kate said, "That sounds great."

"Pick an open site and park this thing. I'll bring the car around to meet you."

A few minutes later, Eddie was holding the door so she could climb into the passenger seat. It was her car, but he was driving. Sam greeted them as they entered the diner. Kate guessed Eddie had let him know they were on their way.

Kate wasn't hungry. She was exhausted. But she enjoyed being back in familiar surroundings with old friends. Eddie held her door again when they got back to the car. As he climbed into the driver's seat, he leaned over and kissed her on the lips. She reached up and grabbed his head and held on for a long passionate kiss.

He said, "Would you like to stay with me tonight?"

Kate recoiled. Eddie said, "I've got two bedrooms."

"The camper is my home. That's what I'm used to."

But as they were pulling into Camp Discovery, she said, "You know, sleeping in a real bed sounds pretty good."

She used one of his clean T-shirts as a nightgown. Her clothes were still packed in the suitcases in the trunk of her car. Something else to take care of tomorrow. She crawled into bed next to him. "No funny business."

"Your wish is my command."

Kate eased back into her old life. She returned to work at St. Elizabeth's. She enrolled in a nursing program that offered online classes allowing her to work full-time. The diner would have to wait until after her baby was born. In the meantime, she began helping Eddie with chores around Camp Discovery.

The couple announced their engagement at a Thanksgiving party. They were married on Christmas Eve. Their son, Gregory Graham Flores, was born on a cold, blustery day in March.

Afterword

MacGregor's Final Battle is my response to a question. Someone wanted to know who would play me if my life was a movie. That's a nonstarter. My life is too boring. But I was intrigued. I came up with MacGregor as my avatar. He has a lot in common with me. He's older, he's retired, and he's had a long marriage.

This is a memoir but it is also historical fiction. It is a fanciful version of what really happened over the period from the 1940s to the 2020s. Mac is five years younger than me. He gets away with a year in Vietnam but he loses everything. As this story begins, he is free to drive across the country and carry on a romantic affair with Kate Graham.

My initial concept of Katherine Graham was inspired by a nurse who had been in high school with my daughter. I consulted with a Facebook friend, Dr. Katherine Fornili, who is not only a nurse but an educator. She suggested Kate's age and troubled background, but we disagreed on the rank. My friend suggested a top-of-the-line Nurse Practitioner. I chose a bottom of the barrel Certified Nursing Assistant, in keeping with the David versus Goliath theme in the story.

I'm not sure how I decided to include Lewis and Clark but it was a good decision. The Trail structured Mac and Kate's journey across the Great Plains and gave me an excuse to pepper the story with historical trivia.

Mac has a cousin in Alaska because I have a cousin in Alaska. I don't think she lives in Fairbanks. Her grandmother and my father got to be friends as children during the Depression. She contacted me after discovering my family tree on Ancestry. We have continued to correspond via email from time to time. I doubt that she is anything like Kirsten Learned.

I'm not sure how I hit upon brain cancer as the monster that would kill Mac. It turned out to be another good choice. I discovered many inspiring memoirs of people who made a valiant effort to maintain normality after learning that they had brain cancer. *The Priority List* by David Menasche was the most relevant. Menasche was teaching high school in Florida when he found out he had brain cancer. At first, he struggled to maintain his normal life. That became impossible. The chemotherapy treatments became so burdensome he decided they weren't worth it. He stopped them. He reconnected with many of his former students through Facebook and eventually arranged to travel around the country as a guest of some of those students. He completed the trip in spite of being virtually blind and otherwise handicapped.

After the trip, he visited his doctors who declared him to be in an amazingly good health. At the end of the book, he was staying with a couple of the students who were still living in Florida. That was all I needed to send Mac on a journey across the country in a camper.

My first attempt at the story was told in first person. Mac was the narrator. When I had to come up with the way to continue the story after he died, I decided to switch narrators. Kate took over after Mac's second stroke in Fairbanks. That version of the story was published on Wattpad and I received some encouraging feedback. But an editor convinced me to rewrite the story in third person. I am happy with that decision and the way the story stands now.

Finally, this book would not be nearly as good as it is without the editorial service of Alicia Anne Creger. Her accompanying commentary was both helpful and delightful.